WITHDRAWN

Brehony, Kathleen A.

Up the bestseller
lists!

$12.95

Up

the
Bestseller
Lists!

A Hands-On Guide
to Successful Book Promotion

Kathleen Brehony & Karen Jones

ADAMS MEDIA CORPORATION
Avon, Massachusetts

Published by Adams Media Corporation,
57 Littlefield Street, Avon, MA 02322
www.adamsmedia.com

ISBN: 1-58062-409-X

Printed in the Canada

J I H G F E D C B A

Library of Congress Cataloging-in-Publication Data
Brehony, Kathleen A.
Up the Bestseller Lists! / Kathleen Brehony and Karen Jones.
p. cm.
ISBN 1-58062-409-X
1. Authorship--Marketing. 2. Self-publishing. I. Jones, Karen M. II. Title.
PN 161 .B695   2001
808'.2--dc21   2001022807

This publication is designed to provide accurate and authoritative information with regard to the subject matter covered. It is sold with the understanding that the publisher is not engaged in rendering legal, accounting, or other professional advice. If legal advice or other expert assistance is required, the services of a competent professional person should be sought.
— From a *Declaration of Principles* jointly adopted by a Committee of the American Bar Association and a Committee of Publishers and Associations

This book is available at quantity discounts for bulk purchases.
For information, call (800) 872-5627.

Table of Contents

Foreword

The idea for this book began one evening over a couple of glasses of wine (a fine Bordeaux, straight from the box). We had both just finished a semester teaching aspiring authors how to write a book and get it published and we were sitting back ruminating over the experience. The one thing that made us shake our heads was the naïveté our students expressed about becoming authors. They simply had no idea that getting published was not an automatic ticket to paradise.

Ergo, this book. We believe it is critical that ALL authors, whether first-time or experienced, know that their active participation in the promotion of their book will, for the most part, determine whether their book will have a shot at being the next bestseller or languish in the discount bins.

Up the Bestseller Lists! was not written from the perspective of an industry insider sitting behind her desk at some gigantic publishing house, instead it was written by two authors, one published by the largest houses, the other by a small publishing company, who have spent time in the trenches trying anything and everything to get their book sold. Therefore, what this book WON'T DO is give you a lengthy and complex view of the publishing industry but what it WILL DO is give you basic, hands-on, practical ways to promote your book. In other words, it will tell you what you need to know, what works, and what doesn't without a lot of verbiage in between. "Just the facts, ma'am."

A cautionary note about the authors: We don't believe in being politically correct, we don't believe in pontificating, and we get tickled at people who believe their own press. We enjoy the absurdities of life, we believe that humor and hard work can get you through almost anything and we both have a rather skewed outlook on life. Kathleen, a clinical psychologist, has had plenty of chances to observe life's oddities and comes by her outlook honestly. Karen's point of view is the direct result of too many years working in rock 'n' roll radio and losing her mind doing television news.

With that caveat in mind, please forgive our indiscriminate use of "he" and "she" instead of the dreaded and cumbersome "he/she." We have also tried to make the book interesting by including our own brand of humor and hope it offends no one. But hey, as Erasmus said: "The highest form of bliss is living with a certain degree of folly."

Read on and prosper.

—Kathleen and Karen

Introduction

Congratulations! If you are reading *Up the Bestseller Lists!,* you are taking a big step toward ensuring the success of your book. Whether you are a first-time author trying to figure out the publishing maze, an experienced author who has seen his well written, well reviewed book languish in the discount bins, or an aspiring author charting out the territory before setting sail, this book is an indispensable guide to helping make your book a success in the marketplace.

But wait a minute! Doesn't having your book published mean getting an extended vacation? You know—resting on a sunny beach in Barbados, sipping frozen drinks, and watching the royalties pour into your bank account? Ah, the fantasy. "Fantasy?" you might say. Yep, fantasy. The very same one we indulged in as we watched the publication of our first books. And the very same fantasy that we saw disappearing into the mists as we realized that birthing a book is a lot like birthing a baby. You've suffered through a long gestation process, delivered this miraculous new life, and shown the baby off to all your friends and relatives. Now what? Now you begin eighteen years (or more) of helping this new life become a real person. So it is with the publication of your book. Your work, in many ways, has just begun.

It's no secret that good publicity is the most important factor in a book's success, and that's just what *Up the Bestseller Lists!* is all about. Think of it as a hands-on, guerrilla publicity manual that can be used by anyone from self-published authors going it alone, to authors supported by a big publishing house who want to take responsibility for their book's success. Our book is fundamental for authors who have to plan an entire promotional strategy themselves, and it is essential for authors who want to supplement their publisher's efforts and keep tabs on what is being done on their book's behalf.

If you are serious not only about writing, but about earning your living as a writer and listing *author* or *writer* on your tax forms when it asks for *occupation*, then you probably realize the world of publishing is extremely competitive. Many wonderful, insightful, beautifully written works go right into the discount bins at price clubs only a few months after publication. On the other hand, bestseller lists do NOT necessarily contain the best in fiction or nonfiction, but rather books that were able to find a market because they were effectively distributed and promoted.

Up the Bestseller Lists! will give you practical and creative ways to keep your book moving toward the bestseller lists, and out of those discount bins! The information we will be sharing with you is based on our experiences as first-time authors. Over the long haul we've discovered what works, what doesn't, strategies to help push your book to the top, and pitfalls to avoid.

It is critical that, as an author, you understand your pivotal role in your book's commercial success. Whether you have self-published your book or published with a small or major publisher, the life your book will have in bookstores around the country depends on your knowledge of effective promotion. We sincerely hope that this book will give you some new ideas, help you avoid crashing into potholes, and afford you a jump-start on your personal and creative venture of promoting and selling your book with enthusiasm and confidence.

1

Books in America

The most important thing for you to understand is the reality of book publishing, both the good and the bad. How many readers are out there? How many books are actually published each year? What is the state of the publishing industry, and will your book have a chance? The answers are the foundation upon which you will build your book's success. Let's get the bad news out of the way first.

Take a look around your home. You see books almost everywhere, don't you? Chances are if you're a writer then you're probably a voracious reader. You have books lying open on the kitchen table, waiting on the nightstand, and tossed across the sofa. There is usually a book or two in your car for traffic jams and several on the back seat waiting to be passed along to friends.

You love the look and smell of bookstores, and a quick glance at your monthly budget shows that a good proportion of your discretionary income is spent on books. You may even believe, like the Renaissance scholar Erasmus, "When I have a little money, I buy books. If there is any left over I buy food and clothes." When you pack for vacation, you are more concerned about what you are bringing to read than you are about the SPF factor of your sunscreen. And like Kathleen, you agreed with the second-grade poster proclaiming "Books Are Your Friends!"

Now look around the houses of most of your friends. (Don't count your writer friends—that's not fair!) Do you see shelves packed and overflowing with books? Are there books tossed here and there waiting to be read? Have they shoved a book in your hands recently and demanded that you simply must read it? We bet we know the answer.

Approximately 60 percent of Americans do not read books at all! In a survey of 16,000 households, the Association of American Publishers and the Book Industry Study Group found that 60 percent of Americans had not purchased a book in the past twelve months. Doesn't that make you cringe? Don't you hope that your friends in Paris won't find out? Of the books purchased, two-thirds were for popular fiction, but even then, further research shows that 57 percent of all books purchased are never read!

Why? One answer may lie in the fact that in this modern age, books compete with television, the Internet, movies, computers, and videos for people's free time. When you consider the rather dismal statistics about America's reading and book-buying habits, just remember the 7.5 hours a day that a television is turned on in the average household. You may wish you had turned to writing television screenplays or multimedia "blow 'em up" computer games for Sony Playstations instead.

Another answer may be the size of the publishing industry as a whole. In spite of the fact that publishing generates $19 billion a year in sales, it is a relatively small industry. Nineteen billion dollars may seem staggeringly high, but this revenue includes all forms of publishing, from children's illustrated books to Bibles, textbooks, dictionaries, and encyclopedias. Trade book publishing—novels and general nonfiction—accounts for only $6 billion a year. According to one source, there are thirty-five American companies that produce more income than the entire publishing industry.

So how many books are actually out there? The United States Copyright Office states that there are approximately 63,000 new titles each year. According to the industry bible, *Books in Print*, there are currently 1.35 million titles and more than 700,000 books currently in print. This presents an overwhelming number of options for the relatively small market of people who read books. Publishing is an extremely competitive industry with a few giants and multitudes of small players vying for a piece of the relatively small pie. The odds of a book generating profit are nothing to bet on. In fact, according to a *Publishers Weekly* survey, only 10 percent of fiction books and less than 40 percent of general trade titles earn back their advances.

What kind of sales can an author expect with these odds? Well, regardless of the literary, entertainment, or information value of a book, the average hardcover by a new author, whether fiction or nonfiction, usually sells fewer than 5,000 copies. Royalties from the sale of 5,000 books won't allow for a vacation to Barbados much less a retirement there, or a dispensation from working a regular job to pay the bills.

Reality does bite, doesn't it? But don't let it discourage you from creating a bestseller out of your book. Rather, let this information light the fuel in your rockets and give you the power to generate active and creative participation in your own success.

The good news is knowledge is power. Trite? Perhaps, but never so true as when promoting your book. Knowledge of the industry will prove invaluable, and it is critical to your book's success. The more you understand about the trends and realities of the publishing industry, the better your chances for making good marketing decisions.

How do you find out about these trends? We highly recommend that you read the major publishing industry publications *on a regular basis.* The Big Daddy of them all—and by far the most important—is *Publishers Weekly,* a weekly magazine brimming with important insider information and reviews for fiction and nonfiction. It is generally, and with good cause, considered to be the bible of professional publishing. Keeping on top of current events in the publishing industry can give you powerful insider information and help you make important decisions by understanding the players who may be able to help you.

Karen is currently shopping her collection of Southern short stories, *The Marcell Glide.* In "Hot Deals," a column in *Publishers Weekly,* she read about five agents who recently made some amazing deals for short-story collections. She sent a query to each one. She also saw an article on book fairs that specialize in romance novels, so she plans to bring copies of her romance extraordinaire, *Kingdom of Hearts,* to the fairs to sell them. The magazine also gives great information on what is selling, strategies bookstores are using to promote books, and current reader trends.

If you want more information about *Publishers Weekly,* you can find it at larger bookstores and well-stocked newsstands. Purchase a copy or two before subscribing. Although a subscription is fairly expensive (about $189 a year), you may be able to split the cost of a subscription among your group of writer friends and share the copies. You may even be able to deduct the cost on your tax forms as a business expense. The magazine is also available in the periodical section of most libraries—check yours out.

To order *Publishers Weekly,* call (800) 278-2991 or visit their Web site at *www.publishersweekly.com*.

So now you know a bit more about the publishing industry and the tremendous competition it engenders. For your book to be successful, it must have effective promotion. This could happen in one of two ways: (1) get selected for "Oprah's Book Club"; or (2) work hard to promote your book and slug it out like the rest of us.

If Oprah chooses your book, you'll join the ranks of Maya Angelou, Wally Lamb, Jacquelyn Mitchard, Sheri Reynolds, and Jane Hamilton and watch your book soar to the top of the best-seller lists. If you personally know Oprah, you can stop reading our book right here. Her impact on book sales is unprecedented—and almost inexplicable. *LIFE* magazine noted that "more than ten million copies of eight serious novels, including Toni Morrison's *Song of Solomon* have flown out of bookstores on Oprah's word."

Every author and publisher in the world would love to be selected as one of her favorites. However, Oprah chooses books for inclusion in her book club based on her own personal likes. Of course, you should send a copy of your book and a press kit to her producers (see Appendix A and B), but unless Fortune should smile at you, you will have to choose the second option: slugging it out with the rest of us.

The Four Ps

Slugging it out involves paying attention to something marketing experts call *The Four Ps*. These elements are basic to this book and your success as an author. Here's a quick example to show what they mean.

Let's say you walk into a store to buy cereal. Your hand reaches for *Captain Crunch*. Why? Because you like that particular cereal? Because it's inexpensive? Perhaps you reach for it because you remember a cute commercial about it, or maybe you are simply in a hurry and it's the first cereal that catches your eye. Welcome to the world of "marketing mix," the realm of professional marketers where—whether selling books, cereal, or soap—they use four basic concepts to ensure successful marketing of their product:

> **Product:** That *Captain Crunch* tastes so good.
> **Price:** And it's cheaper than the others or at least competitively priced.
> **Place:** It was right where you could see it.
> **Promotion:** The commercial was so adorable.

Although you're NOT selling cereal, you ARE selling a book. The operative word here is *selling,* and you need to know about marketing mix in order to develop a successful marketing plan.

The Four Ps are not clearly distinct categories of activity. You will see a great deal of overlap as you consider the importance of each one. You will also see that each concept is filled with opportunities for creative application for the marketing of your book.

These four basic concepts are woven throughout our book. We'll discuss some of the following aspects:

> **Product:** An appealing cover design and enticing title
> **Price:** The reasonable amount of money to expect readers to spend on your book
> **Place:** How to get your book into bookstores and noticed
> **Promotion:** How to get organized and get the word out

So get ready to slug it out like we did! Get hopping and build a plan to promote your book! Grab a pen and underline as you go, adding your own thoughts and ideas in the margins to the ones we are presenting. With your good creative mind and lots of energy and enthusiasm, you will make your book the one that everyone has lying open on the nightstand!!!!

Points to Remember

- Approximately 60 percent of Americans do not read books.
- The entire publishing world generates only $19 billion a year.
- More than 50,000 books are published each year in the United States. (Some estimates suggest that when everything is totaled, more than 147,000 new titles are released each year.)
- There are more than 700,000 books currently in print. (Bowker's *Books in Print* says that there are approximately 1.35 million titles currently in print.)
- The average hardcover by a new author usually sells fewer than 5,000 copies.
- Knowledge of the industry is invaluable, and it is critical to your book's success.
- Knowledge about marketing mix is critical for building an effective marketing plan.

2

Product and Price

Your product is your book and every detail is important. We assume that you have put everything you have into your book—time, money, and effort, not to mention blood, sweat, and tears—and that you have a very good book to sell. From the quality of writing inside to the eye-catching cover on the outside, you should be involved in every important aspect of your book.

Unless you are self-publishing, you probably won't have to decide about things such as paperweight, typeface, and trim size. However, you should still have a say concerning the title and the cover. If your book is not yet printed, we have some very important points for you to consider. If your book has already been printed, perhaps you can use the information for the second printing if your publisher agrees to changes. You can certainly use this information for your second bestseller. Let's take a look at this the way a marketing strategist would.

The Title

Good, catchy titles can make or break a book, and as such, your title is your single most immediate and important sales tool. After all, it is the first thing a consumer (and editors, buyers, and reviewers) will notice. Your title is like a newspaper headline. Subtitles can offer additional information, but your title should be able to stand on its own. It must be a grabber.

Do you remember a book called *Tomorrow Is Another Day,* detailing the life of a dynamic heroine named Pansy? Of course you don't. The title was changed to *Gone with the Wind,* and the heroine was renamed Scarlett O'Hara. Neither Karen nor I can imagine Rhett Butler taking a woman named "Pansy" in his arms and carrying her up those long dark stairs (shiver). Can you? How about a book called *Trimalchio in West Egg?* Would that have found a way into your shopping cart, or would you have more likely bought *The Great Gatsby?* You get the point. Literature is filled with examples of how a simple title change made an enormous difference in a book's marketability and its overall sales.

Karen chose the title *Blood and Heart* for her romance novel. The story was a mix of passion, betrayal, and bloodlines, and she wanted the title to reflect these plots. The publisher, however, said the title sounded like a horror novel, with dripping blood and sliced-up hearts— yikes! After plenty of discussion, much of it heated, Karen agreed to a change, and the title became *Kingdom of Hearts.* It was her publisher's best-selling book of 1997.

Look at your own title. Is it evocatively descriptive and provocative? Can you think of a better one? What book titles have attracted you as a reader (and book buyer)? Make a list of the words in your title. Then go to a thesaurus and find alternative words. See if substituting new words will make your title more powerful.

If you don't already have a title, spend an afternoon cruising through a large bookstore with pen and paper. Write down the titles that draw you to look at the book. Scan the best-seller lists. What seems to sell? Make a list of the "action" words in best-selling titles. Get into a relaxed, right-brain state of mind, the way you do when you write. Meditate for a bit. Ask your higher Self to help with this important part of your writing career. Let the ideas flow, and let images and phrases come into your mind. Write everything down. Don't let your internal critic enter at this stage with its nay-saying comments about how lame that idea is. You can edit later.

Repeat this same procedure with some creative friends and let everything come out. Karen sat down with her mother and sister and came up with a list of twenty-five titles for her pub-lisher to choose from. Brainstorming is the best way to find your fantastic title—you'll know it and feel it when you have the right one.

The Cover

Pretend that you've been invited to the coolest party of your entire life. By a twist of fate you'll have a chance to get down with the likes of Mel Gibson, Julia Roberts, and Will Smith. You will be introduced to these stars as you enter, and you will have all of eight seconds to make an impression. An hour before the party you stand in front of the full-length mirror and study your reflection. Is the hair just right? What about the outfit? Does it say exactly what you want it to say? Will your look attract the attention of Will or Julia (or perhaps both)? Will they, after a brief introduction, find you interesting and intriguing, and want to spend more time with you? Now is not the time to get sucked in by that old adage "you can't judge a book by its cover." Karen says she'd throw on her "to die for" black dress, shove her feet into life-threatening high heels, and be out of the door in a New York minute.

Now pretend it's your book that has the chance to make that big impression, an even more important one. The design and packaging of your book is a critically important component in its effective marketing. This is not only true for books but for all products being sold in a competitive marketplace. American industry understands this and spends $50 billion a year in product design and packaging for everything from cereal to shampoo to doggie treats.

Early in his career, Kathleen's father was the marketing director for *Better Homes and Gardens* magazine. The magazine's research showed that shoppers grabbed 30 percent more copies when there was a picture of a chocolate cake on the cover. No one really ever understood why. Hungry consumers? Rampant PMS? Nevertheless, it was an empirical observation, a powerful correlation backed by sales statistics, and so the editors featured a chocolate cake on the cover almost every month.

Surely you have been in the huge mega-bookstores like Barnes & Noble, Borders, Books-A-Million, and Crown (which has now filed for bankruptcy). In these stores, readers are offered overwhelming choices; most of these superstores stock more than 100,000 titles, each title hoping for the chocolate cake–cover effect. Unless you simply run in to buy a particular book, you will browse shelves in the areas that interest you. Research has shown that approximately 50 percent of customers in a bookstore are there to purchase a particular book, but the other 50 percent are just browsing. These folks can be seen sipping cappuccino and looking around for something that interests them. Furthermore, once in the bookstore, they *will* buy books. And what is one of the things that will attract them to a book? The cover.

Browsers in bookstores look at covers all the time. Don't you? In our opinion, book buyers have a high level of sensitivity about the feel of a book. Cover design is a critically important element in generating first interest. In fact, your book's cover is the most powerful point-of-purchase sales tool that you have. According to research reported in the *Wall Street Journal*, your title and cover have about eight seconds to catch the interest of a potential book buyer—and that's AFTER you've enticed that person to pick up your book.

Fifty-four percent of the browsers will buy one or more books before they leave the store, even though they didn't come in for a particular title. An excellent and intriguing cover is essential for making them pick up, examine, and purchase *your book*.

With all that in mind, you might ask yourself, "Exactly how do I go about getting a good cover?" Unless you have self-published, your publisher will be designing the cover—and it's a good thing, too. Major publishers employ skillful art departments that are charged with creating professional and enticing cover designs, and they will do a better job than you would (unless you are also a graphic artist). In addition to the art department's creative input, your cover design will also be based on the opinions of people in the sales and marketing departments—people who have built their professional lives on understanding how marketing helps to sell books.

You want to take full advantage of the expertise of your publisher. But you also want to have some part in the cover selection process. In your contract with your publisher, ask for "review rights" of the cover. In this case, the publisher designs the cover, but you have the right to make comments and offer opinions. This is important for several reasons. First, it ensures that the cover will not just be thrown together at the last minute since it must be sent to you first. Most professional publishers will stick to a well planned schedule, but it gives you a small margin of insurance just in case. Second, it gives you the right to complain and negotiate if, for some unusual reason, your publisher offers you a hideous cover.

When Karen received the cover of her book *Kingdom of Hearts,* she immediately reared up in protest. The people on the cover looked nothing like the two lead characters: the guy was too young, the girl had the wrong hair color, and what was it with all those breasts, anyway? The publisher, once he could shut her up, told Karen that the characters were designed to get readers to buy the book. He also told her that while she was a very good writer, it was the cover that truly sold the book. And he was right.

For the second printing of her book, Karen had a different publisher and had the luxury of working with the graphic designers, and the second cover was more to her liking. The cover for *Awakening at Midlife* changed rather dramatically from the hardcover to the trade paperback edition. Along with some graphic changes and the addition of a different subtitle, the paperback edition includes some information that was not printed on the hardcover because it was not available at the time of printing. In Appendix A and B, copies of covers for Karen's book *Kingdom of Hearts* and Kathleen's *Awakening at Midlife* are shown in reviews and press materials. This brings us to our next point.

Blurbs

Most blurbs are quotes from notable people (at least, for your particular market) exclaiming what a wonderful book you have written, how they were moved to change their lives by your words, or how you are more powerful than Xena the Warrior Princess. At some time in your life, you've probably purchased a book on the basis of such quotes by another author or someone whose opinion you respect. Quotes can be especially beneficial for new authors who are unknown to the book buying public.

In the case of *Awakening at Midlife*, actor Robert Urich read the book, really loved it, and called from his home to tell Kathleen just that. She, of course, was floored by a phone call from the famous actor, but regained her senses in time to ask him if he would give her a quote. He generously agreed. In fact, he asked for a day or two to write something poetic and special that reflected his feelings about the book. His quote appears on the back cover of the trade paperback.

In addition to offering words of praise, a blurb can present other eye-catching information. Much to her delight, Kathleen was asked to appear on PBS with a televised presentation representing the material from *Awakening at Midlife*. Because the television program was distributed nationally and aired throughout the country, the paperback now includes the blurb "As Seen on PBS." People who have never heard of Kathleen Brehony have certainly heard of PBS, and that brief mention on the cover may be enough for someone to pick it up and look at it for longer than eight seconds.

Of course, the obvious question is, "Where do you get the quotes?" If your book has not yet been printed, it is to your advantage to send galleys or proofs to famous people who might offer a quote. You should work with your publisher to brainstorm a list of people who might have some reason to comment on your book. Don't be shy. Write a respectful letter to each of those people and send a copy of the completed manuscript or, better yet, a bound galley. In your letter ask them for a quote that you can use on your book.

For example, if you have just written the new, great book about unified field theory and the creation of the universe, your book sales would benefit enormously from a nice quote about your brilliance by physicist Stephen Hawking. If you have written a thriller, Tom Clancy's endorsement would be invaluable. Books about alien spacecraft landing in Roswell, New Mexico, would clearly benefit by a recommendation from . . . we're sorry, we won't say who. (We could tell you, but then we'd have to kill you.)

If your book has already gone to press, then keep in mind that subsequent printings can and should include cover changes that make consumers want to pick up the book and buy it. If celebrities or people well known in your subject area are impressed by your book, make sure to ask them for a quote that can be used for later editions.

If your book wins any awards before a second or third printing, you can still include this information on the first edition cover. For example, if you are a National Book Award or Pulitzer Prize winner or even a nominee, you would be foolish not to include this information on your cover. Don't forget about small, regional book awards as well. Publishers and bookstores have stickers for just this occasion. And, after they add the sticker, they often move the books to a special section for easy access.

Price

Economist Adam Smith once noted, "The real price of everything, what everything really costs to the man (sic) who wants to acquire it, is the toil and trouble of acquiring it." While that is very true, the reality of publishing is that it costs money to print a book. Another reality is that you will have little input about the price of your book unless you are self-publishing it. Instead, your publisher will determine the price based on a number of variables. If you do have a publisher, this information will help you understand their reasoning. If you are self-published, the following will help you make a reasonable decision about your book's selling price. Let's take a look.

What Determines Price

The variability in the pricing of general fiction and nonfiction books is mostly due to the fluctuating cost of paper, but it is also due to the book's size and number of pages. The inclusion of graphics or photographs will also impact the final price of a book. "Coffee table" books, for example, are always very expensive because they are printed on costly coated paper stock and usually include color photographs that require four-color printing, sometimes on every page. Some textbooks and others written for esoteric audiences may be very expensive—far in excess of the cost of the paper and production—but then again, how many people are actually going to buy a book about the "Sexual Displays of the Mehely's Horseshoe Bat," with the exception of a handful of graduate biology students?

How Much Your Book Should Sell For

As a guideline, general fiction and nonfiction books of 200 to 300 pages sell for these average prices:

Hardcover: $25.00

Trade Paperback (also called *quality paperback* or *soft cover*): $17.00

Mass Market Paperback (the 4" x 7" editions usually sold next to magazines): $6.00

Note: The average price for a mass market paperback in 1977 was $1.72!

The first printing of Karen's mass market novel was reasonably priced at $5.00. When her publisher told her this, she was completely insulted! After all, she had worked her butt off writing it and felt it was worth more. Later, at book signings, as she attempted to cajole readers into buying her book, she would say, "Oh come on. Five bucks? Buy it! It's a bargain!" and people would do just that. (Actually she bellowed the words as she lunged for readers' shirttails, attempting to drag them into the bookstore. We don't suggest that tactic; we're still trying to have her record cleared.)

Another consideration about the price of your book is the amount of money that will go into your pocket at the end of the day. The higher the price, the greater the royalties you will take home. Now the $5.00 price for Karen's book helped sell it, but think for a moment. If she had been self-published and priced the book at $7.00, she would have made a lot more money, but would it have sold as well priced at $1.00 over the standard mass market rate? As a matter of fact, Karen's book has been rereleased as a trade paperback, and the price is now considerably higher. So are her royalties, but her sales have decreased slightly. If you are self-published, you should carefully weigh what the market will bear against the amount of money you want to take home for all of your hard work.

Author's royalties are most often tied to the price of a book. In other words, your royalties will be a percentage of the cover price of the book. The higher the price of the book, obviously, the higher your royalties, and the sooner you move to Barbados. Industry standards are usually considered to be as follows:

Hardcover: 10 percent on the first 5,000 copies sold; 12.5 percent on the next 5,000 sold; and 15 percent of all copies thereafter

Trade Paperback: 7.5 percent

Mass Market Paperback: 4 percent on the first 150,000 copies sold; 8 percent of all copies thereafter

When we think of price, it is easy to think only about the amount of money your book will cost a consumer, but remember Adam Smith's words: "The real price of everything, what everything really costs to the man (sic) who wants to acquire it, is the toil and trouble of acquiring it." Price includes whatever effort it takes for the consumer to get something. Thus, price also incorporates what your readers have to do to get your book. Do they have to drive to another state to buy it? Do they have to buy it in your garage, where you have stockpiled case upon case of your book? Do they have to place a special order for it—a process that may take days or weeks? Is it easily available on the Internet? This aspect of price leads us to the next issue: place.

Points to Remember

- Good, catchy titles can make or break a book.
- Make sure your title is evocatively descriptive and provocative.
- The design and packaging of your book is critical to its effective marketing.
- Your book's cover is the most powerful point-of-purchase sales tool you have.
- In your next contract with a publisher, ask for "review rights" of the cover.
- Blurbs from famous people can be especially beneficial for new authors.
- You will have little input about the price of your book unless you are self-publishing it. If you are self-publishing, price your book to sell.
- Price reflects the cost of paper and color photos, if any.
- Average prices for books of 200 to 300 pages range from $6.00 for a mass market paperback to $25.00 for a hardcover.

3

Place

Remember the Captain Crunch cereal? It was easy to grab and purchase, wasn't it? That's because it was both in the store and at eye level. In other words, it was easy to FIND—and that is the single, most important issue relevant to place. As an author, you hope that your book is both readily available at all bookstores and displayed in a conspicuous location: in other words, easy to find.

Getting Your Book into the Bookstore

About a third of the bookstore market is controlled by three major booksellers: Barnes & Noble, Borders/Waldenbooks, and Books-A-Million. In addition, Hudson News Company is heavy in airport shops throughout the United States. Obviously it is critical that your book is carried by these major bookstores. We've listed their addresses, phone numbers, and Web sites here.

Barnes & Noble
122 Fifth Avenue, 4th Floor
New York, NY 10011
Phone: (212) 633-3300
Web site: *www.bn.com*

Borders/Waldenbooks
201 High Ridge Road
Stamford, CT 06904-3417
Phone: (203) 968-9700
Web site: *www.borders.com*

Books-A-Million
402 Industrial Lane
Birmingham, AL 35211
Phone: (800) 201-3550
Web site: *www.booksamillion.com*

Hudson News Company
1305 Patterson Plank Road
North Bergen, NJ 07047
Phone: (201) 867-3600

If you are working with a major publisher, the sales reps will certainly sell your book to the major booksellers. But if you are working with a small publisher or have self-published, you must get your book into these stores yourself. Before we tell you how to do this, we want to emphasize that it is important to work cooperatively with your publisher. Be sure to let him know who you are targeting and how you are contacting people. That said, the best way to reach these major booksellers is by contacting distributors and wholesalers and urging them to carry your book instead of calling the bookstores directly. How do you do that? Read on.

Wholesalers and Distributors

The distribution of books is a complicated process that often skips steps and uses overlapping terms. In order to keep from either boring you to death or confusing you, we offer this simplified explanation.

Books begin their journey to bookstores at one of two places: a main distributor or the publisher. It is here that books are warehoused, and it is here that the main distributor or publisher tries to market or sell the book to wholesalers, specialty distributors, regional distributors, retailers, and so forth.

Wholesalers, specialty distributors, and regional distributors purchase books from the main distributor or publisher, and provide fast and efficient restocking services for independent booksellers and, sometimes, the large chains. Wholesalers also provide advertising options to publishing houses (though usually not for specific titles). Specialty and regional distributors provide advertising too, but their marketing is more extensive, and they will attempt to generate orders for specific titles.

The two largest national book wholesale companies for fiction and general nonfiction are Ingram Book Company and Baker & Taylor. Ingram is the largest wholesaler to independent bookstores in the country. Ingram offers next-day delivery to more than 95 percent of its bookstore and library customers, and it serves more than 18,000 bookstores and libraries. You can contact Ingram at the following address:

Ingram Book Company
1 Ingram Boulevard
LaVergne, TN 37086-1986
Phone: (615) 793-5055
Web site: *www.ingrambookgroup.com*

Baker & Taylor offers bookstores a listing of more than 100,000 titles and 10,000 forthcoming titles. They are the largest distributor to libraries throughout the country, stocking more than 3 million books and 120,000 titles. You can contact them at the following address:

Publishers Contact Services
Baker & Taylor
2709 Water Ridge Parkway
Charlotte, NC 28217
Phone: (800) 775-1800 or (704) 357-3500
Web site: *www.btol.com*

You can look up other wholesalers and national distributors at your local library in *The American Book Trade Directory* or *Literary Market Place*. These are the professional reference books for the publishing industry. You can purchase one for $250. Both books are published by R. R. Bowker and can be ordered by calling 888-BOWKER2 or contacting their Web site at *www.bowker.com*. These reference books are gold mines of information about the publishing industry and, if you can afford them, are among the professional writer's major tools. However, most libraries have copies of the *Literary Market Place* or *The American Book Trade Directory* in their reference section.

In addition to the two big wholesalers, there are other natural distributors that can offer your book to bookstores. Most of

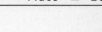

the companies in these books are members of the American Wholesale Booksellers Association at (*www.awba.com* or 219-232-3143). Here is contact information for five of the largest companies:

Koen Book Distributors
10 Twosome Drive, P.O. Box 600
Morristown, NJ 08057
Phone: (800) 257-8481

Bookazine
75 Hook Road
Bayonne, NJ 07002
Phone: (201) 339-7777

The National Book Network
4720 Boston Way
Lanham Seabrook, MD 20706
Phone: (301) 459-3366

Alamo Square Press
4530 18th Street
San Francisco, CA 94114
Phone: (415) 863-7410

Partners
2325 Jarco Drive
Holt, MI 48642
Phone: (517) 694-3205

In marketing your work, you should also target regional distributors for the areas where you live or where you will be visiting for book signings and personal appearances. Regional distributors work in the major geographic regions: eastern, middle, and western. Each of these regions are broken up into smaller ones. Bookstores, especially the independents, usually have strong relationships with these companies. You can get a list of regional distributors for your target areas by calling a major bookstore in your location and asking the manager about distributors.

You should also contact specialty distributors if they distribute books in your genre or area of interest. For example, New Leaf Distributing Company is by far the largest national distributor for New Age and metaphysical books and magazines. Their catalog has more than 300 pages and is sent to booksellers and New Age stores throughout the country. Therefore, if your book would appeal to New Age readers, you certainly want it to be available through New Leaf Distributing Company. You can contact them at:

New Leaf Distributing Company
401 Thornton Road
Lithia Springs, GA 30122-1557
Phone:(770) 948-7845
E-mail: *newleaf@newleaf-dist.com*
Web site: *www.newleaf-dist.com*

There are specialty distributors in many different genres and categories of books. Talk to your publisher or call the kind of bookstore that carries books like yours. For example, there are quite a few specialty bookstores throughout the country that only carry mysteries, business books, Christian books, literary fiction, and so forth. Call them. Ask what distributor(s) they use to get books. Then contact those distributors.

If you are working with a major publisher, you should send a personal flyer describing your book to the major wholesalers, distributors, and your personally targeted regional and specialty distributors after your publisher's marketing department mails them its fall and spring catalogs and before your publicist sends your book's press kit. (We discuss personal flyers and press kits in Chapter 4.) If you are working with a small press, most of them usually have a tight budget and can only send out fall and spring catalogs to wholesalers and distributors. If that is your situation, you should follow up their mailing with a personal flyer and a press kit, being sure to also contact your targeted regional and specialty distributors. If you are self-published, find out when the fall and spring catalogs are being sent and send your personal flyer and press kit to the major wholesalers and distributors and your personally targeted regional and specialty distributors yourself.

Getting Your Book Noticed in the Store

Most major bookstore chains have clearly defined procedures for where books will be placed in their stores. Independent bookstores generally have greater latitude in placing books where they want. It is important to get to know the people in your local bookstores—both independents and chains. It has been our experience that booksellers are a friendly bunch and love to meet new authors. In addition, they are more likely to set up book signings (more on that later) and "hand sell" books when they've met and like the author.

A cautionary note: Not every chain or independent bookstore is receptive to author phone calls. Although these stores usually like to set up signings, some have been besieged by overzealous, first-time authors who want a daily accounting of sales or pester for special favors. You might want to ask local authors or writers groups about their experiences with the bookstores. If you find a bookstore that does not like phone calls, drop the manager a friendly note explaining who you are, what your book is about, and what you would like to do. Be sure to include your address, phone numbers, and e-mail, and wait for them to contact you.

If you decide it is appropriate to call a local bookstore, use good sense and your best manners when you approach them. First, find the appropriate contact person. Large chain bookstores usually have a position called a CRC—for Community Relations Coordinator (sometimes called CRM, Community Relations Manager)—who is responsible for setting up author book signings.

Don't make a move until you've confirmed that you've got the right contact person. Both store managers and CRCs are busy people, and excited authors can sometimes appear aggressive and pushy without meaning to. You might want to call to ask if you can make a brief appointment or offer to buy the manager a cup of coffee. When you meet the store manager (or CRC), it is important to let him know that you are excited and will help in any way, but that you also have realistic expectations about what the store can do for you. Remember, you are selling yourself as well as your book, and nice guys (and gals) finish first.

If you just happen to be in a bookstore, don't expect the manager to drop everything just to talk to you. Politely introduce yourself, ask how sales are going, and offer to sign a few copies of your book. This is a very good idea. Not only do you get to practice signing your name, but once you have signed a book, it generally cannot be returned!

Remember, be polite, use your common sense, and know when to take "no" for an answer. It can go a long way toward smoothing the path for your next book signing, and that of the authors who follow in your footsteps.

Whenever possible, connive, intrigue, and tap-dance to get your book placed on the "New Release" shelf or table when it is first published. Even small bookstores dedicate an area for brand-new fiction and nonfiction books. This area has great visibility, is located in the highest traffic area, and usually can be found in a location that you must pass when you first enter the store. We will go into more detail about just how to do that tap dance with a discussion of the Bookseller Boogie in Chapter 4.

Kathleen's brother, J. P., found *Awakening at Midlife* on a front table at a large Borders bookstore in northern Virginia. He was delighted that her book was on the premier table, one that all customers had to pass as soon as they entered the store, but he was not thrilled that his sister's book was placed at the back of that table. He asked the manager to move Tom Clancy's *Executive Orders* to the back and shift *Awakening at Midlife* to the front, citing his interest in social justice and believing that Tom Clancy was doing well enough on his own. To his great surprise, the manager was happy to do so and excited that a local author had a book in his store. Not all bookstore managers will be this compliant and helpful, but availability and placement are critical considerations.

How critical? In food marketing, for example, manufacturers pay considerable "bonus fees" to supermarkets to have their products placed on shelves at eye level or on endcaps, where they are readily seen by consumers. It is hard to for us to believe that consumers won't bend over to pick up the Cheerios they want if a Wheaties box is right in their direct line of sight (it makes us seem like mindless robots), but years of psychological and empirical analysis of consumer behavior clearly indicate that placement is a critical consideration in buying decisions. This is also true in book sales. In fact, major publishers will often pay a special co-op fee to get certain kinds of prime placement in bookstores, like those cardboard end-caps that contain numerous copies of the hot new novel. Still, some bookstores can make decisions about whether they will place new releases on the "New Release" shelves or on a table near the entrance of the store.

Kathleen did several book signings at Manteo Booksellers, a small, wonderful independent bookstore in Manteo, on North Carolina's Outer Banks. Steve, the manager, and several others who worked there got to know her and like her, and they loved *Awakening at Midlife*. More than a year after the hard-back publication date, her book continues to be displayed on their front shelf—the most desirable placement in the store—displaying employee "favorites." The manager and staff there have taken the time to get to know their regular customers' likes and interests, and they "hand sell" her book and many others. Each time they tell customers that they've read it and loved it, more royalties come in.

Getting Your Book Noticed in Other Locations

Approximately 56 percent of all books are purchased at book-stores, and your distribution through them must be effective. On the other hand, you don't have to be a statistical wizard or even the sharpest knife in the drawer to figure that 44 percent of books are purchased in locations other than bookstores. In addition to obtaining books through libraries or borrowing them from friends, people buy books through book clubs and at drugstores, supermarkets, airport gift shops, newsstands, and chain discount stores. But there are even more creative locations for book sales.

Of course, the old idea of "shotgun" marketing—sending the message out to as many people as humanly possible—is no longer regarded as a viable option. It's simply too expensive to promote a book to an inappropriate market. Instead, professional marketers speak of *narrowcasting* instead of *broadcasting*. This idea, called *target marketing,* focuses all marketing efforts on the specific populations that are most likely to be interested in your product: in this case, your particular book. In order to effectively market your book, two questions should always stay in the front of your mind:

1. Who will buy my book?
2. Why will they buy my book?

Think about your target market. For example, if you have written a book about hiking the Appalachian Trail, you can reach a more significant number of potential readers by getting your book in front of that specific target market: in this case, making sure your book is placed in stores that sell hiking and backpacking equipment. A cookbook will probably find a powerful market niche in a store that sells fancy kitchen gadgets and copper cookware. A book about cats could sell very well in a pet supply store.

Our friend Evelyn has written a wonderful novel that is set among characters involved in NASCAR racing. Her book will benefit from being placed in catalogs that cater to those interested in this sport and at places where tickets to these events can be purchased.

Further evidence of target marketing can be seen at Starbucks. This chain of coffee shops has included a rack filled with books that have been selected for Oprah's Book Club. It is believed that people who wish to linger over a steaming espresso are likely to pick up and buy books recommended by Oprah. The thinking is apparently correct. Starbucks is selling "tons of books," according to our small, personal survey of a half-dozen stores. Always remember: *Target marketing is a critical point to understand in order to effectively market and promote your book.*

Karen has sold hundreds of copies of *Kingdom of Hearts* to conventions and groups interested in the romance genre. Kathleen attended a Judy Collins outdoor concert and, recognizing that the entire audience was made up of middle-aged people, kicked herself for not renting a kiosk next to the beer stand. You get the idea. Think creatively. Who do you believe will be buying your book? What is your target market? How can you effectively reach them through nontraditional means? Write all these ideas down so you don't forget any. In fact, we urge you to write a specific marketing plan that includes all of your creative ideas for nontraditional or special locations in which your book would sell.

Getting Your Book
Noticed in Cyberspace

The Internet is rapidly becoming one of the most popular forms of information sharing today, and it offers remarkable opportunities for marketing your book. Most major publishers assert their presence by having their own Web site on the Internet. And, according to a 1998 study conducted by Nielsen Media Research and CommerceNet, books are one of the hottest items being purchased through e-commerce. This study showed that

5.6 million people have purchased books online. Although this is not a comprehensive list of every nook and cranny in cyberspace where your book can have a presence, we do have a few ideas to get you started.

Internet Bookstores

Today, more and more Web sites are those of "regular" bookstores that have an extra location in the ineffable world of virtual reality. Your book should be included in their inventories. If you are a cyber traveler, go to any search engine, type in "booksellers," and you will be given a list of thousands of booksellers offering to sell their products online.

In many cases, an Internet bookstore will show your book cover, provide detailed information about its contents (if nonfiction) or a detailed story line and description (if fiction), and offer you, the author, a chance to respond to an online interview. Some sites even offer opportunities for authors to communicate directly with readers through "live chats."

There are too many Web sites to name here, but they sell millions of dollars of books every year. One of the best sites for you to explore is *www.amazon.com*. Named after the South American river, this bookseller claims to have more than one million titles that can be shipped within two or three days, and another 1.5 million copies of hard-to-find and out-of-print books that can be shipped within weeks. They claim to have "earth's biggest selection" and are very helpful. They do a very nice job of providing author profiles and plugs for books.

You should also check out *www.barnesandnoble.com,* an online cyber version of their superstores.

A good place for you to begin your search is the online bookstore information site *www.buyersindex.com/brca/12.htm*. This site gives an annotated list of 350 key sites. And don't forget

specialty online bookstores that cater to genre markets, such as
www.crimepays.com, the online Partners & Crime Mystery
Booksellers; or *www.sirenbooks.com,* the online romance fiction
bookstore. For the book you are reading right now, we checked
out Scribe and Quill at *www.scribequill.com*. This online
resource and community site for writers has a great bookstore.
We're excited that Scribe and Quill has agreed to review our
book, and we're hoping it will be available on their site.

Your Own Web Page

Nothing announces your presence on the Internet better
than having a site of your own. It is from here that you can
advertise your book, communicate with browsers, take orders if
you are self-published, and create links to related sites online
and e-bookstores that carry your book. It's really not as complicated or as expensive as it might seem. Some net servers provide
a simple home page as part of their basic service. Other net
servers will charge a nominal fee for you to establish your home
or Web page. As for getting listed on the Internet (so browsers
can find you), most search engines like Yahoo, Excite, Lycos,
HotBot, and Infoseek are happy to list your Web page for free.

Before you decide to establish a Web page, it's a good idea to
browse through cyberspace to see how others are using their Web
pages to make an impact. Once you decide to have your own Web
page, you can do one of two things.

First, you can hire someone to design your Web page. This
service is becoming more and more affordable as time goes on.
Find an interesting and effective Web page on the Internet and
send them an e-mail asking who their designer is. Both of us are
only modestly computer literate. Nevertheless, even young
children set up Web sites for purposes far less grand or important than your book. (One of our favorites is a site consisting of

16,000 haiku dedicated to the lunchmeat Spam; see *http://pemtropics.mit.edu/~;cho/spam/*.) The monthly cost of maintaining a Web site has come down tremendously in the last year or so, and the technical skills necessary for setting one up have gotten easier and easier. Check with your Internet server to see if it offers a Web site as part of your subscription.

In addition, there are many excellent instructional books about how to set up a Web site and relatively simple software programs that can help you do it. Two books that have gotten rave reviews are:

> *The Non-Designer's Web Book: An Easy Guide to Creating, Designing and Posting Your Own Web Site,* by Robin Williams (no—not "the" Robin Williams). Peachpit Press, 1997. This book offers an introduction to design principles for beginning Web users and is geared to the person who has no background in design or the Web.

> *Web Design in a Nutshell: A Desktop Quick Reference,* by Jennifer Niederst. O'Reilly & Associates, 1998. This book offers helpful tables and lists and also provides information in understandable, bite-size servings.

If you do decide to have a Web page, remember that you must incorporate compelling design, audience evaluation, clear communication of site content, and effective advertising. It's a good idea to check out different Web pages for ideas. To start your research, find a good Web ring, a group of related Web sites, that focuses on your topic or genre. Karen's forthcoming romance novel *The Highland Witch* takes place in Scotland, and she has been checking out Scotland Web rings for good ideas for her Web page. To find a good Web ring, simply go to *www.webring.org/index.html#ringworld*, and you are on your way. If you do not have the confidence to establish a Web site on your own, we are certain that you have at least one brilliant geek friend who could help you do this. Now is the time to call in your chips.

Marketing Online

Establishing an active business presence on the Internet can also be an option depending on your situation and needs. Authors working with a major publishing house shouldn't need this, but if you are self-published or working with a publisher who is asking you to do most of your promotional work, this may be an option for you. The Internet can provide an aggressive and active marketing presence to help sell your book. For ideas about selling your book online, take a look at:

> *Guerrilla Marketing Online Weapons: 100 Low-Cost, High-Impact Weapons for Online Profits and Prosperity*, by Jay Conrad Levinson. This book offers, among other things, information on planning and organizing your marketing strategy, advertising, publicity and free information, special events, and customer comfort.

> *The Internet Marketing Plan: A Practical Handbook for Creating, Implementing and Assessing Your Online Presence*, by Kim M. Bayne. This book is a bit more sophisticated and offers information from formulating marketing communications strategies, to designing advertising and direct mail campaigns, to planning your Internet marketing budget.

Other Online Options

The first places you should go on the Internet are the online bookstores that already list your book. The most obvious are:

Amazon: *www.amazon.com*
Barnes and Noble: *www.bn.com*
Borders: *www.borders.com*
Books-A-Million: *www.booksamillion.com*
Alpha Craze: *www.alphacraze.com*

You might want to go to a search engine and type in your book's title. You will probably be astonished at the number of online bookstores that have your listing. Look at each online listing of your book. Most will include a picture of the cover, publishing information, a brief description of the book, a brief author bio, a place for author comments, and a place for reviews. Be sure the description is correct, and check the accuracy of your author bio.

Most of this information is supplied to the online bookstores by the publisher. If you want to change any of it, you should talk to your publisher first. Not every site will have all of these features, but the larger bookstores have most of the information. These larger bookstores will also have author programs that give their authors the opportunity to participate in live chats, list upcoming signings, write comments about their book, add links from their book's site to their personal Web page or other online review sites, and receive e-mail from readers.

Cyberspace is expanding daily, and so are your opportunities for marketing. Now is the time to surf the World Wide Web. You never know where the next wave will take you. For instance, did you know that the Science Fiction and Fantasy Writers of

America (*www.sfwa.org*) will promote your first book by posting your banner on one of their pages for a month for free?

How about looking for news groups that might have an interest in your subject? Simply go to search sites such as *www.egroups.com, www.topica.com,* or *www.onelist.com* to find online groups just waiting for your words of expertise!

There are many more ways to make your presence known on the World Wide Web that are quick, fun, and inexpensive:

- Take a look at Web sites you have bookmarked as relevant to the topic of your book. These sites often have such events as online seminars and contests.
- Join chat groups that have an interest in your subject matter. Identify yourself as an expert or, at the very least, as an author who has just written a book on the topic.
- Regularly tune into discussions about books and creative writing at the numerous sites devoted to these topics (e.g., *www.salon.com*).
- Get online with a newsgroup. This is where you can post notes about your book and keep your readers updated.
- Join an online writing group.
- Be on the lookout for daily new events to join. For example, on one occasion Yahoo! listed the following events: Coffee Time International Book Chat; The Writer's Pen (chat for published, unpublished, or aspiring writers); Fantasize! (chat about sci-fi or fantasy books); and many more.
- Check out sites that specialize in promoting on the Web.

In this day of consumer advertising overload, your book MUST be up front and center. This means making sure your book is available through the major wholesalers and distributors and the regional and specialty distributors. This also means making sure your book is prominently displayed in bookstores, creative alternative locations, and cyberspace.

Points to Remember

- If you are working with a small publisher or have self-published, you have to get your book into bookstores yourself.
- The best way to reach bookstores is by contacting distributors and wholesalers and urging them to carry your book.
- The two national book wholesale companies are Ingram Book Company and Baker & Taylor.
- National distributors who can offer your book to bookstores are Koen Book Distributors, Bookazine, The National Book Network, Alamo Square Press, and Partners.
- Be sure to also target *regional* and *specialty distributors*.
- Get your book placed in the store on the "New Release" shelf or table.
- Forty-four percent of books are purchased in locations other than bookstores; target these locations.
- The Internet is the most popular form of information sharing today and offers remarkable opportunities for marketing your book.
- Announce your presence with your own Web site.
- Establish an active business presence on the Internet.
- Make sure your book is included in online bookstore inventories.
- Surf the Internet to find other ways to market your book.

4

Promotion

Turn on the television, and you see an author on a talk show. Flip open the newspaper, and you find an ad for an author coming to town for a lecture. Walk into your local independent bookstore, and they are giving out bookmarks with each sale. From a spot on a national talk show to a lecture in a coffeehouse, promoting your book is critical. The greatest impact on the success of your book occurs when you become intimately involved in the process of its promotion. Will you have fun? Yes. Will you get a chance to be wildly creative? Yes. Will the majority of the time be spent in hard work and follow-up? You bet! And the payoff is worth every second of it. Successful promotion of your book depends on your ability to jump in, do the work, and cooperate with those people in the position to help.

If your book has been published by a major publisher, you will be assigned a *publicist*. In fact, usually there will be a staff of people who are charged with promoting the books offered by that publisher. This support is an important benefit of publishing with a major house. But, do not believe that even with a major publisher, the publicity department will do everything required to effectively market your book. At the same time, if you are working with a publicity department, it is important not to get in their way. Make sure you are aware of what they are doing on your behalf, and don't duplicate their efforts.

If you are a new, midlist, author, it is unlikely that you will be given the time and energy that will be devoted to known authors who are expected to deliver bestsellers. If, on the other hand, you are Patricia Cornwell and have received a $24 million advance from Putnam for three books, you don't need to read any further. Just get on the plane and go to the talk show that has been scheduled for you. For the rest of us, the publicist will want our involvement with our book's promotion.

Keep in mind that this person, or this team of people, are working hard to promote a number of books. You *must* be involved, and you must keep abreast of what is happening with the promotion of your book. When you work with a publicist, it is important that you have a good relationship and excellent lines of communication. Kathleen and I both feel strongly that it is important for you to have at least one face-to-face meeting, even if it is inconvenient and you have to travel to New York (or wherever) for a single meeting. Your effort will be worth the trouble. Yours will no longer be just another book on a long list of books to be promoted. Instead, you will be a real person and have a real relationship with the team of people working for the success of your book.

If you are self-published or working with a small publisher, your involvement will be essential to the success of your book. You may not be assigned to a specific publicist but handed over to a member of the general marketing division. Large budgets are usually lacking in such situations, so here is your opportunity to save the day with your enthusiasm, creativity, and willingness to work hard.

Whether you have a big-time publicist, are with a small publisher, or are self-published, the following information will help you make your book the success that you dreamed of.

Getting Organized

The only way to keep track of everything that will happen with the publication of your book is to be completely organized—at least, as organized as you can manage. We aren't suggesting you become a total anal retentive, but taking on some of those qualities wouldn't hurt.

Create an Amazing Filing System

If all goes well, you will have a great deal of paper to deal with. Since you've written the next bestseller, you will be overwhelmed with reviews, feature stories, letters, and other material related to the promotion of your book. But where are you going to keep all that stuff?

Karen wanted everything kept in one central place: a place that would never change, a place where everything could be readily found. She cleared out several drawers of a filing cabinet in her writing room.

If you want to be a little more flexible and be able to move the information from room to room or perhaps to your car, you can buy a plastic file box and a new bunch of file folders. Kathleen preferred total mobility and used a large three-ring notebook with plastic sleeves so she could carry her promotion materials around with her, taking her materials to meetings and interviews. As you begin to acquire articles about you and your book, file each one in a separate file folder for your drawer or in a plastic sleeve if you decide to keep things in a notebook. Be sure to keep all originals in a safe place. Use a Post-It note to designate each one as the "original," and don't ever give it away—ever. Chances are good that you will be making copies for press kits and other promotions, and the best reproductions will come from these originals. No matter how you decide to become organized, be sure to do it before the deluge hits!

Hang a Monster Calendar

Planning a promotional strategy can be confusing, with many overlapping deadlines. The best way to avoid this confusion is to have a huge wall calendar so you can see the entire year in front of you. Go to your local office supply store and buy a large laminated wall calendar that shows the months of the year in spacious blocks. Make sure you buy at least three different colored pens that can write on the surface clearly and also be wiped off. Start by writing in dates that you know. These dates should include:

1. When you have to mail the flyers to the distributors so they get them right before the sales kit arrives.
2. When you have to send galleys or copies of the manuscript to reviewers in order for its review to come out with the book's release.
3. When the publisher will send their marketing department's sales kit to distributors.
4. When your book will be published.
5. When your book will hit specific stores or will be available to ship.

We know this sounds complicated, but it is easier to plan if you can see it in front of you. Becoming accustomed to using this kind of planning device early in the process of promoting your book will be very helpful as you begin to book dates for interviews, book signings, and so forth. If you are working with a major publisher and have been assigned a publicist, that person will be responsible for mailing galleys and books to reviewers and sending information to distributors. However, you still need to know what is going on with your book and where you are in the process.

Don't Leave Home Without the Dreaded Day Planner

We know. You want to be an artist, an author, not a yuppie, but how do you think all of those Beemer drivers got their money anyway? They crammed as much into each day as they possibly could. To do that, you need a day planner that is portable, something you can carry with you and refer to at all times.

Obviously the weekly/daily calendar can be used for reminders and appointments. The section that will be most helpful is the back of the book where you can make your own sections. We suggest that you use these sections to keep track of the following:

Your publisher: Log all calls from your publisher, noting the date of the call and what the call was about. Note any follow-up activity and put it on your to-do list.

Book signings: Use one page per signing. List contacts, dates, names, supplies needed, and any follow-up required, including the thank-you note.

Media: You can divide this into television, radio, and print. Be sure to subdivide these sections into local, regional, and national categories. Again, one per page is fine.

Agent: Yes, you still have to deal with your agent, and we hope you are working with one you respect and trust, because an agent can be a good source of creative ideas. Be sure to log all calls and note what your agent is doing or not doing to help you publicize your book. This will help you decide if you want to use this agent for your next bestseller!

Producing the Premier Press Kit

If you are working with a major publisher, your publicist will develop a press kit that will be sent along with a copy of your book to hundreds of reviewers, feature writers, and radio and television producers. If you are working with a small publisher or if you are self-publishing, you will have to develop your press kit yourself.

A press kit is a simple, portable way of telling a producer, reporter, or reviewer about you and your book. It should look professional and be appealing. Remember that this is your book's way of saying "hello," and the press kit should get attention and create interest. It is such an important part of your marketing plan that you should carry several copies with you at all times. We suggest sticking a few in your car and your office if you work away from home. You never know when you will need one.

If you are preparing the press kits yourself, spend a few extra dollars to purchase good-looking, high-quality folders (with inside pockets) from an office supply store. Use quality paper for your reprints and descriptions. It will be worth it in the long run. There are lots of other places to skimp and save in promoting your book. You can stay at fleabag hotels and eat lots of sand-wiches when you are on your book tour, but putting together a cheap press kit is not a smart way to save.

Once you have a nice folder, ask your publisher for extra copies of your book cover and glue a copy to the front of each folder. This is an inexpensive way to make your press kit really eye-catching and professional.

So much for the outside. Now, using the same high-quality materials as you did for your cover or folder, include the fol-lowing in your press kit:

1. **A letter or press release** introducing you and your book. In most cases this will be signed by the pub-lisher and be printed on their stationery.
2. **A one-page author bio** that describes you and any interesting and pertinent details of your life.
3. **A brief summary** of book.
4. **A 5" x 7" glossy black-and-white photo** of yourself. Use a professional photographer, and stress that it must be a headshot done in black and white. (If you had one taken for your book cover or jacket, you can just use it again.) The photo should be reproduced to include contact information—usually your publicist or publisher. If you are self-publishing, use your own name, address, and phone number. Keep the original negative and one original print in a safe, dry place. We hope you will need to go back for many more reprints.
5. **Photocopies of any reviews or articles that focus on you and/or your book.** Again, take the time to make these reproductions look clear and professional. Type—don't write—the name of the newspaper and

date of publication. Spend some time at your local photocopy place to make these look fabulous.

6. **A list of questions that media people can use.** You want them to be able to interview you without doing a lick of work, because the easier you make it on them, the more they'll appreciate you, and the better they'll make you look.

7. **A copy of the book cover** if you didn't use it on the cover of your press kit.

8. **A copy of your business card and/or bookmark.**

Appendix A and B show some of the material we included in each of our press kits, such as author bios and press releases. Use your imagination, but make sure the items we've just listed are available in your finished product.

Get Some Great Business Cards and Bookmarks

When you are out and about talking with people, a business card is a great leave-behind item that will remind them of your book and of having met you. Business cards can be made on your own computer or ordered from a print shop for a modest fee. Be sure to include your name, the name of your book, and other pertinent information.

In addition to business cards, many authors have found that bookmarks can serve as a valuable marketing tool. Bookmarks can be another way to get your name and your book in front of the public eye. Prices for printing them vary according to your design and how many colors you use. Be sure to check with several printers to get the best deal. The front of the bookmark should be splashed with the most eye-catching part of your book cover or with some flashy artwork. The title of your book should be at the top and your name at the bottom. On the back, include a short summary of the book, a list of any other books you have written, your name, and the publisher's name and address. Give each bookstore that will be receiving your books fifty of these, and have plenty on hand to give away at your book signings.

Getting the Word Out

So you're organized and have press kits galore. What's next? How about letting people know about your wonderful new book. Here's how.

The Author's Questionnaire

Your publicist will want to know a great deal about you in order to target reviewers, media, feature writers, and producers who might be interested in your book. You will be asked to complete an "author's questionnaire" as your publicist plans the marketing strategy. The questions are designed to look for hooks that will be of interest to reviewers and the media. By examining the answers to these questions, you and your publisher will have a better idea of where to send promotional material (Karen's author questions are reproduced in Appendix A, page 180). Feel free to create one of your own so you can find your own personal hooks for targeting the media.

Karen wasn't assigned a publicist, so she had to make her own list. Luckily, she was working in television news, so it was easy for her to compile her list of hooks for potential reviewers and others in the media. If you weren't assigned a publicist or if you are self-published, ask yourself about when you can do book signings or shows, whether or not you have any media contacts, and topics you can speak about that pertain to your book. These questions will help you structure your thinking about your book's promotion.

Answers to your author's questionnaire can provide powerful promotional ideas. For example, if you were the first baby born on New Year's Day in Philadelphia in 1961, local readers might still be interested in what you are up to now, even though you've been living in Kalispell, Montana, since you were six months old. Thus, sending a press kit and review copy of your book to the *Philadelphia Tribune* makes more sense than just throwing a dart at a map of the United States and looking for cities to market. If you once danced professionally, especially as an exotic dancer at an after-hours club close to the White House, there will certainly be interest in Washington, D.C., about your new career as a writer. When you send your book for review or send your press kit for a possible interview, your cover letter should emphasize your local connection.

If you went to school at the University of Virginia, both the academic community and Charlottesville residents will certainly be interested. If your fiction takes place at UVA, even if you've never set foot on the grounds of the university, there is still likely to be interest on and around the campus. After Anne Rivers Siddons's book *Outer Banks* was published, you could find copies of it for sale all over the Outer Banks of North Carolina. Not only bookstores but drug stores, restaurants, and motels had racks of this mass market paperback for sale; the assumption was that residents and tourists would find a novel set in this locale to be of interest.

Remember, all of the questions in the author's questionnaire are designed to help you and your publicist discover ways to develop interest and make you, as an author, and your book stand out from the crowd. It is important that you take the time to complete this questionnaire yourself.

Six Degrees of Separation

Do you remember John Guare's hit Broadway play, *Six Degrees of Separation*? (Yes, there was a play before the movie with Will Smith and Stockard Channing and even before "Six Degrees of Kevin Bacon.") The play is a farce based on the popular idea that there are only six degrees of separation, six people, between any two human beings on Earth. For example, a homeless man on the streets of New York City knows a social worker who knows a priest whose cousin is an alderman in Chicago who dates an assistant producer who works with Katie Couric.

We can't prove the theory, but we do know that if you want to get your book into the right hands, you must use every resource you have. You never know where the next great lead will come from, so it's important that you think creatively, and tell everyone you know about your book. You never know who they know, and who those people know, and on and on.

Karen was lucky enough to work in television news as a feature reporter, so she had good access to famous people. She sent *Kingdom of Hearts* to singer Michael Bolton, with whom she has remained friends since a 1991 interview. She also sent a copy to a distant cousin in Los Angeles, Vince Gilligan, who is a writer, producer, and director for the *X-Files* and who made *Entertainment Weekly*'s July 1998 list of "The 100 Most Creative People in Entertainment." All it takes is for your book to be on the table and the right person picks it up and you are off on your fantasy adventure. Just think, if Karen's cousin knew someone who knew Spielberg and because they both loved the *X-Files* they accepted an invitation to her cousin's house for dinner, and then *Kingdom of Hearts* was lying on the coffee table and Spielberg picked it up—oh baby, oh baby!

Celebrities aside, other contacts are good too. Karen has kept in touch with a friend she met years ago while living in Princeton, New Jersey. During their most recent, yearly phone update, she found out that this friend's best friend is vice president of the children's books division at a major publishing house. Yowza! Talk about a contact!

We also know someone whose sister is married to a guy who plays tennis with the cello player in Lyle Lovett's band! So see? You never know!!!

But how do you capitalize on your own six degrees of separation? We recommend making sure that all of your personal contacts know that you have published a book. We mean everybody. We're talking your first-grade teacher here. The most important thing you can do is make the reading public aware of both you and your book. All of the regular avenues for publicity are fine, but to make your personal "six degrees of separation" work, you must ask yourself two important questions: (1) "Who do I know?" The answer is likely to be more people than you think! And (2) "What do I know?" Let's look at the first question.

Who Do You Know?

Make a list of the people you know: parents, relatives, friends, friends of friends, doctors, dentists, lawyers, members of your church, members of any club you or your parents or friends belong to, people you went to school with, people at work. These are people who will buy your book, help spread the word, and be happy to tell others that they know a published author. Ask them to tell their own friends about your book and to ask those same friends: (1) if they will spread the word; and (2) if they know anyone in the media or in the entertainment business. Now is not the time to be shy. Who knows, perhaps one of your friends has a friend who knows a producer on *Good Morning America!*

Also, if you do not belong to a writer's organization, now is the time to join. We have found fellow writers very helpful in spreading the word and helping to make contacts. These writers and your other friends can post flyers, help you think of creative ways to publicize your book, and most important, *call bookstores and ask for your book!* Bookstores pay a great deal of attention to callers, so get everyone you know to call in, even before your book is published. The sound of your title ringing in booksellers' ears may encourage a bookseller not only to place an order for your book, but also to order a few extra copies when they do so. Just make sure you don't annoy the bookseller. That could certainly spell disaster.

Right after Karen's book was published, her parents drove across the country. Every time they stopped in a town, her father would go to the local bookstore and tell them he was looking for her book! What a guy!

Similarly, Kathleen's business partner, Caren, and Caren's husband, David, travel extensively and love to browse art museums and bookstores. They have made it a point to always ask about Kathleen's books, complimenting the store manager when they are available and, particularly, when they are well displayed. They have taken photos of her books in stores from Seattle to Florida, a campy little collection.

Kathleen also assembled an extensive Christmas card list that included more than 250 names. Realizing that calling each of them, especially people she hadn't talked to in a long time, was a daunting, unrealistic task, she made a personal flyer and mailed it to everyone on her list. With today's computers, it is simple to make up a mailing list and mailing labels, and send a flyer, folded and stapled, for only a small investment. Even if you don't own a computer, you probably have a friend who does. If not, then most large photocopy centers have them available for a small fee.

Remember, don't be shy about making these contacts. Even celebrities do it! In the mid-1990s, Karen was sent to Los Angeles to interview several celebrities, one of whom was Suzanne Somers. A month later, Karen received a ThighMaster (remember them?) in the mail from Ms. Somers. The letter graciously began, "With no preconceived notions of your physical needs . . ." Ms. Somers went on to thank Karen for the interview and request a copy of it. At the same time, she cleverly promoted her ThighMaster. Everyone in the newsroom tried it out, and several people bought one! What a great promotional idea! Now, on to the second question.

What Do You Know?

Your topic, of course! If you have written a book about motorcycles, the president of the Harley-Davidson club would be interested in it. If you have written a book about the state of race relations in 1990s America, Julian Bond would most likely want to read it. No matter what your book is about—formula racing cars, sailing, battered women, exceptional children, health alternatives for the terminally ill—find famous people who are interested in that topic and send a copy of your book to them. For example, Walter Cronkite loves to sail, Shirley MacLaine loves to be reincarnated, Michael Bolton has a charity for disenfranchised women and children, Michael Keaton loves to hunt and fish, Bill Cosby is interested in education, Paul Newman races cars, Joanne Woodward adores the ballet, Mary Tyler Moore works tirelessly for diabetes organizations, Robert Redford is committed to cleaning up the nation's rivers. If you have written a fiction book that is plot driven, look at the other elements in your book. If your story is set in the Florida Keys, send a copy to Jimmy Buffett. If your book is set in Richmond, Virginia, in the 1950s, send a copy to Warren Beatty, who went to high school there. If you have a mystery set in the fashion industry, send a copy to Donna Karan. You get the idea: think about what you know from popular culture.

We advocate a very assertive but respectful approach to sending copies of your book to celebrities. We call this dynamic tension between aggression and esteem "just short of being a used car salesman." Always use publicly known addresses for the celebrity. Understandably, they get really spooked if you use their home address. Find the name of a studio or television network associated with the celebrity, get the telephone number through information, and call for the proper address. If you are trying to find information on recording artists, call the local radio station that plays their music and find out the musician's record label. Sometimes the radio station will have a phone number for the label. If they don't, just call information in New York or Los Angeles and you should get the label's main number. For those of you interested in country music artists, simply call the Country Music Association in Nashville at (615) 244-2840.

If you use the Internet, this process is easier still. Just go to a search engine and type in the name of the person you are interested in. By going to the Web sites identified, you will be given more information than you will ever need. The addresses listed there will often include the agent, producer, or television/film/recording studio associated with the person you are looking for. And be sure to keep an eye on your local entertainment calendar. Celebrities who may have an interest in your book, musicians on concert tours, or actors touring in shows may be coming to a venue near you. If you want to give celebrities a copy of your book while they are in the area, you can do one of two things. First, you can call the radio or television station that is sponsoring the event and ask to be included in a backstage "meet and greet" and give the book to the celebrity then. Or, you can call the promoter (who is always listed at the bottom of the newspaper ad) and ask how you can get the book to the star. As a rule, promoters won't tell you where the artist is staying (for very good reasons), but they will probably let you bring your package to them and they will see that it is delivered.

Once you have your celebrity addresses, make up your package. Include an appropriate cover letter to introduce yourself. Sign the book and send it, but don't expect a reply. You should also realize that sometimes the book will not be properly delivered.

But don't let that discourage you. If you don't try, you'll never succeed! Karen attempted to get on MSNBC with radio disc jockey Don Imus. It didn't happen, but the point is, it could have! The exposure would have been super. Here is a paragraph from her letter to him. If you are familiar with Imus, then you will recognize that she wrote using the language he uses on his show.

> I think it would be a hoot to visit your show and defend the romance genre. All you would have to do is read the book (it won't hurt and it won't turn you into a girl, I promise) and we could chat on-air about your reactions. So many people give romance writers grief and say that they could write such a book blind-folded. Well, I am here to testify that writing a novel is harder that it looks and besides, I would like people to know that not all romance readers and writers live in double-wides.

Since there are no hard and fast rules, follow your own instincts and intuition about sending press kits, a copy of your book, or other information to celebrities. If you have been published with a major publisher, work closely with your publicist, who will probably be happy to send copies of your book to people you think might have an interest.

As we've mentioned, Kathleen decided to send a copy of *Awakening at Midlife* to actor Robert Urich. She had seen him being interviewed by Diane Sawyer shortly after he was diagnosed with cancer and was touched by his courage and honesty. Kathleen believed that he would "get" her book and that the message could, perhaps, help him on his journey. She sent *Awakening at Midlife* from the urgings of her heart, not expecting any response or benefit. As it turned out, Mr. Urich was very impressed with the book, called her to tell her so, and wrote these words for the cover of the paperback edition:

> TRUTH is necessary in the pursuit of knowledge. KNOWLEDGE mixed with insight and love leads to wisdom. WISDOM is God's gift. You will find all three in Kathleen Brehony's book.

Karen has written a collection of Southern short stories, *The Marcell Glide*, that she is trying to get published. She wrote them while she was living in Princeton, New Jersey, and listening to the music of James Taylor. His songs of Carolina helped ease her homesickness for the South and helped set the mood for her Southern writing. In 1997, Karen was able to finagle a quick backstage meeting with Mr. Taylor and give him a copy of the unpublished manuscript as a thank you for his inspiration. Now, it would be nice if that gesture helped her get *The Marcell Glide* published, but that's not the point. She gave this copy to James Taylor hoping that her stories would give him as much pleasure as his music has given her.

You, too, can do those kinds of things out of the goodness of your heart. Send copies of your book to people who would enjoy it or learn from it. Send copies of your children's book to a children's hospital, not to get something, but to give. The karmic wheel turns all the time. In book marketing, as in life, the path with heart remains the right road when asking the Universe for its blessings.

Getting Your Book into the Store

Now that you've investigated your own personal six degrees of separation and have your contacts, what about your readers? Your book is due on the shelves soon, and you want the readers out there to buy it! How do you get them to do that? One way is to make sure the book gets into the store.

How does that happen? Remember our earlier discussion about wholesalers and other distributors? These are the people who choose which books to buy from the main distributors and publishers and who distribute their choices to the bookstores. How do they choose the books? They receive thousands of sales kits from hundreds of publishers and from all of that information, they select which books to distribute. It's just like playing pin-the-tail-on-the-donkey. Do you remember, in your younger years, being blindfolded and having to search for the donkey poster on the wall? (If you're still doing this in your adult years, we're sure there's a book in it.) You waved your arms out in front of you and hoped to find something familiar that would guide you to the donkey. Wholesalers and distributors play that same game. They are dealing with so much information that they need something familiar to guide them to their choice. It's up to you to provide that familiar something. What might that be, you ask? The answer, of course, is the fantastic flyer!

The Fantastic Flyer

As we told you earlier, publicists with major publishing houses send personalized letters of communication to wholesalers and distributors along with a slick catalog describing the books on their spring and fall lists. Additionally, their sales departments work closely with distributors' reps to sell your book to them. Remember, if this is the case with your book, you should send a fantastic flyer to the major wholesalers and distributors after the catalog has been mailed and before the sales department sends out your book's press kit. In many cases, small publishers may not have the staff or resources to do this. If they only send out an initial catalog, or if you're self-published, you should send a flyer to each of the major distributors after your publisher's initial catalog mailing (and then follow up with your press kit if you want).

What does this flyer look like? Well, if you want it to be a *fantastic flyer,* it should contain the following:

- Your name and the title of your book at the top in large print
- A picture of you (look cool—but funny is good too)
- A picture of your book cover
- A short summary of your book
- A short bio
- A list of what you are doing for publicity
- Your name, title, publisher, and publication date at the bottom

You want your name and the title to jump out at these people so when they get the sales kit or press kit, which will follow, they recognize it and feel comfortable with the information. If they are NOT receiving a follow-up sales or press kit, they will be reminded that they saw your book in a recent catalog. We know what you're thinking here. Yes, flyers are an expense, but it's worth the price if it gets a major distributor to make sure your book is readily available for the book buyers at Barnes & Noble to order.

Don't forget, the major distributors also have a big say in the choices made by non-bookstore outlets, such as airport vendors and supermarkets. We'd be more than happy to have our books fly the friendly skies or be bagged next to the pot pies! Remember, you can write off the expense once you're making money on your book. In addition, keep in mind the barter system. Do you know a photographer who needs a resume written? Do you know someone with access to a printer who needs a few rooms painted? How about a graphic designer who could use a weekend away from noisy children? You get the drift! Now get the flyer!

So, you have a plan of attack for the wholesalers and distributors, and you know when to send them your fantastic flyer. Now, what do you do about the booksellers? Yes, we know, you have your friends furiously calling Barnes & Noble asking for your book, but you need more than that to get their attention! You need them to WANT your book and to call their distributor and ask for it. You also have to make sure they want to put your book up-front-and-center when it arrives in their store. That's when you proceed to do the Bookseller Boogie.

The Bookseller Boogie
Send the booksellers the same flyer you sent to the distributor. There's no rule that says you can't schmooze them both! The Internet is a good way to find local stores and a description

of each. You can do this by using almost any good search engine. We use *www.iwon.com* and search the "city guides" for "retail bookstores." Santa Fe has 39 bookstores; Baltimore has 64; Butte has 5; and Phoenix has 94. If you really want to set your mind whirling, check out the New York City listing: 334 stores! That's what we mean when we suggest that you read each description carefully before sending a flyer. There's no sense wasting a stamp sending a flyer for your new murder mystery to a children's bookstore!

When you send the flyer to bookstores in your local area and those you are targeting for your author book tour (more on that later!), be sure to include a very nice, chatty, comfortable cover letter that contains the following:

- Who you are
- What the book is about
- How you are advertising/promoting the book
- How eager you are to do book signings
- A list of any radio, magazine, and television appearances you have set up (or the fact that you would like to do so in conjunction with a book signing at their store)
- A list of materials you can supply for the signing: bookmarks, an author photo, posters
- Ideas (just one or two) to make the book signing interesting: a raffle where people sign up to win a free book, a pre-signing question-and-answer period, or a short talk about your book
- An excerpt from your book

Follow up this mailing with a phone call to the manager of each bookstore, again keeping in mind that while booksellers like to arrange book signings, some are very leery of author calls, and some do not like calls at all. It is a good idea to contact a local writers group in the area and find out which stores respond well to author contacts. Remember, these people are usually quite busy, so be polite, pleasant, and to the point. If they seem frazzled, politely offer to stop by at their convenience to chat, or offer to call back at a better time. Your relationship with the booksellers is crucial, and sometimes an author's enthusiasm can be misinterpreted as insensitive or aggressive. They have the power to place your book anywhere in the store they want. It can go at the front of the store, in an eye-catching display, or it can linger in the back room propping up an unstable table leg. It's up to you.

You also want to send this material to the buyers who work for the national chains. You might want to forgo making follow-up calls to national bookstore chain buyers. As a group, they tend to be protective of their privacy. You might want to add a brief, polite note to your flyer, letting them know you will be happy to accept their collect call if they have any questions. We bet this will get you further than being just one more author on the than phone.

Sending flyers and personal letters to booksellers is fine, but what about personal contact, the eye-to-eye variety? It's hard to drop by a Santa Fe bookstore for a chat when you live in Virginia Beach. Eye-to-eye chats work in a limited area, but what if you could meet hundreds of booksellers and go eye-to-eye in one fell swoop? Welcome to the world of trade shows!

Trade Shows

The American Booksellers Association (ABA) was established in 1900. This trade organization exists to protect the well-being of book retailers and to promote the availability of books. This association represents the interests of booksellers at the national and international level through its commitment to education, research, political action, and dissemination of information. Members of the ABA include independent book-stores, franchises, college and university stores, chains, libraries, and others with an interest in book sales.

As an author, you will be happy to learn that the ABA sponsors BookExpo America (BEA) every year in Chicago (usually the first weekend in June). This event is NOT open to the public and is for the trade only—booksellers, librarians, book retailers, book distributors, literary agents, publishers, and so forth. The national convention is overwhelmingly huge and is a place to meet with the people who can make or break your future.

If you are working with a major publisher or even a small publisher, the company will probably have a presence there in the form of an exhibit booth, which will contain copies of your book. It's important to know that the emphasis in these shows is on *future* books. Many authors are disappointed by all the big posters and displays for forthcoming books when their book is nowhere to be seen. But the media covers these events for local and national television and radio. There are many opportunities to get your book seen. Authors also conduct workshops and book signings. Generally the publishers *give* the books to the booksellers, so no royalties for you. But who cares? Imagine, as a brand-new author, having your book seen by hundreds of booksellers.

Even new authors will have hundreds of people lined up to receive a signed copy of their book—after all, it's free! Furthermore, the ABA convention gives you, as an author, a chance to meet, face-to-face, with people who have the power to "hand-sell" and promote your book to their customers. Wouldn't you be more likely to talk about and promote someone you've chatted with? Booksellers are the same. When a customer comes into a store looking for a mystery, the bookseller will be inclined to mention, "I just met this new author who was so nice. We've got a few copies of his book right here." In other words, you are no longer just a name and a title among thousands. Talk to your publisher about getting an invitation to autograph books, or even better, presenting a workshop or a reading at the national ABA convention. Find out about ABA by contacting:

American Booksellers Association (ABA)
828 S. Broadway
Tarrytown, NY 10591
Phone: (800) 637-0037,
or in southern New York: (914) 591-2665
E-mail: *info@bookweb.org*
Web site: *www.bookweb.org*

Note: If you have Internet access, the ABA Web site is very well constructed. It has lots of information and a searchable database that lists more than 4,000 bookstores. It also offers all the details on upcoming conventions and meetings.

In addition to the national association, the industry has generated nine regional booksellers' associations that sponsor conventions, trade shows, and book fairs. These organizations also provide excellent opportunities to meet with thousands of book retailers and distributors. Although very well attended, they are not as overwhelming as the national convention but still offer multiple opportunities where you can meet people who will be directly responsible for selling your book to bookstores and the general public. The following list highlights the nine regional associations, with the name of the city where the convention was held in 2001 and the contact person for that year. Most of the regional associations hold their trade shows in the early fall (September and October). *Publishers Weekly* is a good source of information about upcoming events and usually covers such details in their August issue. Although the contact people are subject to change from year to year, the person who answers the phone will help you locate the correct contact for the current year.

Pacific Northwest Booksellers Association (PNBA)
2001 Trade Show: March 17–19, Couer d'Alene, ID
Thom Chambliss
317 W. Broadway, Suite 214
Eugene, OR 97401-2890
Phone: (541) 683-4363
E-mail: *info@pnba.org*
Web site: *www.pnba.org*

Northern California Independent Booksellers Association (NCIBA)
2001 Trade Show: Oct. 5–7, Oakland, CA
Hut London
5643 Paradise Drive, Suite 12
Corte Madera, CA 94925
Phone: (415) 927-3937
E-mail: *office@nciba.com*
Web site: *www.nciba.com*
*Trade shows always held in Oakland.

Great Lakes Booksellers Association (GLBA)
2001 Trade Show: Sept. 28–30, Indianapolis, IN
Jim Dana
P.O. Box 901
Grand Haven, MI 49417
Phone: (800) 745-2460 or (616) 847-2460
E-mail: *glba@books-glba.org*
Web site: *www.books-glba.org*
*This trade show is held in a different city every year. Considering rotating among Indianapolis, Cleveland, and Lansing.

Upper Midwest Booksellers Association (UMBA)
2001 Trade Show: Oct. 5–7, St. Paul, MN
Sue Walker
5520 Park Place
Edina, MN 55424
Phone: (800) 784-7522 or (952) 926-5868
E-mail: *UMBAoffice@aol.com*
Web site: *www.abookaday.com*
*Trade shows always held in the Twin Cities area.

Mountains and Plains Booksellers Association (MPBA)
2001 Trade Show: Sept. 14–16, Denver, CO
Lisa Knudsen
19 Old Town Square, Suite 238
Fort Collins, CO 80524
Phone: (970) 484-5856
E-mail: *lknudsen@mountainsplains.org*
Web site: *www.mountainsplains.org*
*Trade shows always held in Denver.

New Atlantic Independent Booksellers Association
2001 Trade Show: Oct. 6–7, Washington, D.C.
Carla Cohen
Politics & Prose Books & Coffee
5015 Connecticut Ave. NW
Washington, D.C. 20008-2024
Phone: (202) 364-1919
Fax: (202) 966-7532
E-mail: *carla@politics-prose.com*
*Trade show held in Washington, D.C.

New England Booksellers Association (NEBA)
2001 Trade Show: Oct. 5–7, Boston, MA
Rusty Drugan
847 Massachusetts Avenue
Cambridge, MA 02139
Phone: (800) 466-8711 or (617) 576-3070
E-mail: *neba@neba.org*
*Trade show always held in Boston.

Mid-South Independent Booksellers Association (MSBA)
2001 Trade Show; Sept. 6–9, Oklahoma City, OK
Joe Holmes
2309 NW 120th St.
Oklahoma City, OK 73120
Phone: (405) 751-5681
E-mail: *midsouthbooks@juno.com*
*Trade show is in New Orleans every other year, rotates to
different cities (in the region) in intervening years.

Southeast Booksellers Association (SEBA)
2001 Trade Show: Sept. 21–23, Memphis, TN
Wanda Jewell
2730 Divine Street
Columbia, SC 29205
Phone: (803) 252-7755
E-mail: *sebajewell@aol.com*
Web site: *www.sebaweb.org*
*Trade show is adopting a new Southwest-to-Northeast axis. Trade show was held in Nashville, TN (1996); Mobile, AL (1997); Jekyll Island, GA (1998).

In addition to the ABA and the regional booksellers associations, many other book fairs and specialty events are scheduled throughout the country and the world. You should actively seek out information about these events, where you could have opportunities to market your book. Check the ABA Web site on the Internet (*www.bookweb.org*) for a partial listing of events. For example, the following book-related events have been held (to name only a few):

- Eighth Annual Baltimore Antiquarian Book Fair
- Seventh Annual Dayton Book & Paper Show
- Baltimore Books Festival II
- The Southern Festival of Books
- Seventh Annual Mid Atlantic Mystery Book Fair & Convention
- The International Book Fair Monterey
- Texas Book Festival
- Sixteenth Annual Southeastern Wildlife Expo
- The Virginia Festival of Books
- Bouchercon 29 (The World Mystery Convention)

- The International Map Trade Association Map & Travel Products Trade Show and Conference
- The Frankfurt Book Fair
- The Bahrain International Bookfair
- The Christian Booksellers Convention
- The American Library Association Convention
- The National Association of College Stores

Also be sure to talk to bookstore owners and consult with other writers in your genre. You may be missing promotional opportunities that are right in your own backyard.

In addition to trade shows and festivals that are specifically directed toward publishing and the book-selling industry, think creatively about your book topic and its marketing potential. For example, if you have written a travel book, you might consider becoming a vendor (perhaps with your publisher) at trade shows directed toward the travel industry, such as the International Travel Industry Expo. A children's book might get excellent attention at a toy show or convention. If your book is about boating, you should contact The Mid-Atlantic Boat Show. If you have written a self-help book about some aspect of human behavior, you should consider offering your books for sale (and perhaps giving a talk or workshop) at the American Psychological Association. There are thousands of trade associations in the United States, all of which offer excellent opportunities to put your book in front of very specific market segments—the target market with the greatest interest in your book.

Most libraries have reference books called *National Associations of the U.S.* (also called the *Encyclopedia of Associations*) or *National Trade and Professional Associations of the U.S.* Each of these volumes lists and gives information about trade and professional groups. Plan to spend an afternoon at your library to make an extensive and creative list of groups that might demonstrate an interest in your book. Let the librarians know what you are looking for. They usually have wonderfully creative suggestions. While you're at it, you should become familiar with the trade publications of any industry or group that you have identified as part of your target market. These may also offer opportunities for small, well placed ads that can be a cost-effective way of reaching your market.

Public Speaking

So you've written a book. Does that make you an expert? Sure it does. Think about it for a minute. If you have written a non-fiction book, then you must be something of an expert on your subject. If you are a fiction writer, then you are an expert, at the very least, on your particular story, setting, and characters. You can use this expertise in several different venues to both promote your book and, in the instance of public speaking, actually sell copies.

Speaking in front of an audience is an excellent way to promote your book. Public speaking is a multibillion-dollar-a-year industry in the United States. Many people, experts in their fields, make lucrative incomes by addressing groups with keynote talks and by presenting workshops. As an author, you too can also find remarkable ways to promote your book by giving talks and seminars.

Seminars are a big business in the United States and throughout the world. In fact, a recent study found that more than 40,000 seminars are presented each year throughout North America and generate between $100 million and $160 million. These opportunities to address the public can both generate income and give greater publicity to your book. Some major writers began their careers by promoting their books with seminars and workshops. For example, several New Age writers—Louise Hay, Deepak Chopra, Shakti Gawain, and Wayne Dyer—put together a tour of twenty-five cities, and each seminar drew about 3,000 people. At $50 per ticket, each event generated $150,000. Beyond that, more than $30,000 worth of books were sold at each seminar, grossing yearly sales of more than $4.5 million.

As a writer, you may not yet have the audience of a Deepak Chopra or Shakti Gawain, but there are still plenty of opportunities to speak publicly. If you are a professional in your area of interest, you might want to consider being represented by a speakers bureau. These organizations operate much like literary agents: they will represent you for a commission. The average commission for these services usually runs from 15 to 20 percent. But what does a speakers bureau do? A speakers bureau markets you and your expertise to all kinds of organizations looking for keynote speakers and seminar leaders on a wide range of topics.

Perhaps you don't feel qualified yet to charge a fee for people to hear you speak. You can begin to get the word out about your book and sell some copies by offering your services for free to interested groups. Contact the high school and college or university you attended. Educational institutions love to have one of their own return to speak about a book they have published; it reflects favorably on the school. Librarians love published authors too and would probably be delighted to have you speak at their library. Also take a look around your local area. Every community has a variety of professional associations, service clubs, and business and community groups that love to hire speakers for luncheons and meetings. Often, these groups can only offer a small honorarium or a token gift. We call this the "rubber chicken circuit" after the notoriously bad lunches we've had in pursuit of both publicity for our books and the very nice Cross pen-and-pencil sets we get as gifts.

We do have drawers full of these gift pens and pencils, but you know what else? We sold books. Most authors who speak at these gatherings make more money on "back of the room sales" of their books at the event than they ever make from speaking fees. Remember, if you do speak for free, you should be able to deduct a reasonable "speaker's fee" for that event from the income generated by your book. Be sure to check with your accountant about this!

Learn about the organizations in your community. Even these small speaking engagements will give you valuable experience and set in motion your movement toward becoming an "expert" in your field and feeling confident as such. These events are the groundwork required to move up the ladder to larger, more profitable speaking engagements. Most local newspapers provide listings of various meetings throughout the area. Also, check with your local Chamber of Commerce for listings of such organizations. If you live in a city that hosts regional meetings for professional associations, talk to the managers of local hotels to find out what groups will be holding meetings there during the next six months or so. Contact the program chairperson for those groups. Let the chairperson know that you are an author and an expert on a subject that has a relationship to the group's profession or interest. Ask about getting on their agenda. Make sure you will be able to offer your books for sale at this event. Often these groups have exhibitor areas and will give you a small space to conduct a book signing after you speak. Even if you speak for free, you will most likely sell some of your books.

For example, Kathleen was invited to give a keynote address to a statewide convention of school nurses. Most of the attendees were women. The vast majority were in midlife and, as a result, at the book signing following her speaking engagement, she sold and signed more than 300 copies of *Awakening at Midlife*.

If you are addressing a large group and you anticipate large, sizable sales, contact a local bookstore and ask if they will work the event with you. An opportunity to sell 300 hardcover books is no small thing—especially for an independent bookseller—and most will jump at the chance. Working with a bookseller saves you the hassle of ordering and schlepping books all over the place, not to mention making correct change while trying to chat with potential book buyers!

Even for small events, you can order books through your publisher (with your author's discount) and sell them yourself. Karen has done this several times and has had great success, but she is completely hopeless at making change. She suggests that you look at the cost of your book, figure in the tax, and then round the number to the next highest dollar amount. Making change for a $6.00 book is much easier than handling money for a book selling at $5.78.

Books That Can Help

There are a great number of books available about public speaking both as a business and a skill. Familiarize yourself with these. Three that we like in particular are:

Secrets of Successful Speakers, by Lilly Walters. McGraw-Hill, Inc., 1993. This book reveals the 11 easy-to-follow steps for successful public speaking. It provides useful exercises and gives great tips, including how to handle hecklers.

How to Speak Like a Pro, by Leon Fletcher. Ballantine Books, 1983. This step-by-step guide to successful speaking is detailed and funny. It includes a handy checklist for each chapter.

Speak and Grow Rich, by Dottie Walters and Lilly Walters. Prentice Hall, 1989. This book provides excellent information about venues, fees, speakers bureaus, and speaker agreements. A must-read for public speakers.

Karen is also quite fond of a snappy little book of irresistible and easy-to-use quotes (e.g., Groucho Marx's "Whoever called it necking was a poor judge of anatomy"). Here's a good one to try:

2715 One-Line Quotations for Speakers, Writers & Raconteurs, by Edward F. Murphy. Gramercy Books, 1996.

Additional Tips for Success

Here are some more things to keep in mind for a successful public speaking experience

Before the Event

Once you have confirmed your speaking date, send a formal letter of brief introduction about yourself to the person planning the event. Be sure to include your bio or curriculum vitae and any interesting or pertinent information.

Double-check to make sure your books will arrive in time.

Go to the bank and get change. Karen brings at least $100 worth of $1 and $5 dollar bills with her to speaking engagements. Although that might seem like wishful thinking, usually every bit of that change is needed.

Make a nicely printed stand-alone sign with your name, the title of your book, and the price. Some people are shy about asking.

Things to Take with You

Take a copy of your introductory letter with you. This will be quite helpful to the person introducing you. It also ensures that the most salient details of your background or accomplishments are presented to the audience.

Have copies of your book available for sale. Plan to spend time autographing them for people who buy them. Arrive early and set up your books. There is nothing so awkward as having to drag books out of boxes and toss them on a table while people are crowded around you, picking them up and asking you questions.

Don't forget to bring a small box or pouch filled with correct change, and the stand-alone sign for your table.

During Your Presentation

Always have a copy of your book with you on the platform, and be sure to mention it in your presentation. Prepare a short but powerful talk on one or two main themes. Don't try to cram too much into your talk—the audience can buy your book for the details. Be stimulating. Leave plenty of time for questions and answers. Most professional speakers agree that an audience likes to leave with "the sound of their own voice ringing in their ears."

Publicity

If you are speaking at an event that is newsworthy, make sure that press releases have been sent to the local print and electronic media. Long before your speech, you should be working with the program chairperson to see what can be done to promote the event or at least get news coverage.

Bring ample copies of business cards or bookmarks that mention the name of your book. Distribute them to everyone who attends.

If you are self-published or working with a small publisher, have blank order forms available for those who might want to purchase a book later. Also, add some of the major points from your talk or a list of resources on your order form. This becomes an important "leave-behind": a reminder of who you are, your talk, and your main points.

Self-Promotion: An Example

Remember that many best-selling books were originally self-published and driven to success by the hard-working authors who spoke to groups and booksellers about their work. There is no reason why you can't do this too.

Getting the word out is simply a matter of hard work and using what you already know. For instance, if we had just written *Gone with the Wind*, the great Southern novel set in Atlanta right before the Civil War, the first thing we would do is fill out the author questionnaire to get good ideas about both our topic and ourselves. What do we know? If we have written a book about pre–Civil War Atlanta, we know the Old South.

Next, we would contact all of our friends and acquaintances by phone, flyer, or e-mail to ask if they know anyone who is connected to television or radio and if they know anyone famous (or semi-famous) who is interested in Southern history circa the Civil War era.

Our next step would be to brainstorm about celebrities to whom we could respectfully send a copy of our book. The first and most logical choice would be mega-star Elton John, who lives in Atlanta and who absolutely loves it there. Kim Bassinger might be a good choice. At one time she actually bought a small town in Georgia. Ted Turner would be another logical person to try. He is, after all, the biggest thing to hit Atlanta since Sherman, and you never can tell what he will decide to support. The topic of our book would probably interest country singers too. We'd get online at the County Music Association Web site, read biographies and send a copy of the book to folks like Loretta Lynn and Vince Gill. We'd also send a book to Tommy Lee Jones and Sandra Bullock, both of whom own a ranch in Texas.

While one of us was busy sending copies of our book to celebrities, the other would be looking on the Internet for descriptions of the eighty-nine bookstores in Atlanta. Once we decided which stores would carry our novel, we'd address our fantastic flyers and drop them in the mail. We'd be sure to note in our dreaded day planner when to make those follow-up calls.

Our next step would be to go online and look for trade shows. The *www.bookweb.org* site lists the ABA convention where we could hawk our book, and it also lists the trade show for the Southeast Booksellers Association that is usually held in Atlanta! A must for a visit. We would also find the date for BookExpo America. This is the convention that the entire book industry shows up for.

Public speaking would be our next focus. We would contact the Heritage Preservation Association, the Atlanta Genealogical Society, and the Georgia Sons of Confederate Veterans to see if they wanted us to talk about our book.

We would give a call to the English and history departments of Bauder College, Emory University, Mercer University,

Morehouse College, and Spelman College to see if we could arrange a book signing and give a talk to students interested in history, writing, or both!

Our next move would be to contact museums to see if they would like us to pay a visit. We would also try to have our books sold at their sites. We would target the Margaret Mitchell House, Atlanta History Center, Atlanta International Museum, Fernbank Museum of History, Atlanta Preservation Center, and Wren's Nest, the museum home of Georgia author and journalist Joel Chandler Harris.

Remember, the success of your book depends on getting organized and getting the word out. Promote, promote, promote!

Points to Remember

- The success of your book depends on promotion.
- Know what your publicist is doing, work in concert, and don't duplicate efforts.
- If you are self-published or working with a small publisher, your involvement will be essential to the success of your book.
- The only way to keep track of everything that will happen with the publication of your book is to be completely organized.
- Set up a filing system, hang a wall calendar, and use your day planner.

Points to Remember,
continued

- Your press kit should get attention and create interest.
- Business cards and bookmarks remind contacts of your book and get your name and your book in front of the public.
- The author's questionnaire is critical for planning your marketing strategy.
- Tell absolutely everyone you know about your book.
- Find celebrities who might be interested in your book and send a copy to them.
- Send a flyer to each of the major distributors and book-sellers.
- Your relationship with the booksellers is crucial.
- Talk to your publisher about attending national trade shows.
- Also attend regional booksellers' associations trade shows.
- Investigate trade shows catering to the subject matter of your book.
- Public speaking is an excellent way to promote your book.
- Consider being represented by a speakers bureau.
- Consider offering your services for free to interested groups.
- Don't try to cram too much into your talk.
- You will probably make more money on "back of the room sales" than from speaking fees.
- Make sure you have plenty of books and money to make change.
- Remember to send press releases to all media.

Advertising

All new authors fantasize about seeing a full-page ad for their book in the *New York Times Book Review*. There it is—in full color, with a great description, blurbs from major reviewers, and a terrific picture of you as an "Exciting New Author." What a great idea. But the odds are, it's not going to happen. "Why?" you ask. Well, it has to do with the economic reality of advertising.

Publishers and Advertising

You may never see that wonderful full-page ad because the publishing industry balks at spending money advertising new books. They will spend money advertising a new book by one of their major, best-selling authors, but even then, they are really just notifying the author's regular readers that there's a new book ready for purchase. There are a number of reasons that publishers rarely advertise. First, advertising is enormously expensive. The costs of running ads in print and electronic mediums can shrink a marketing budget in a matter of days. Books are considered a "low ticket" item with a small profit margin, and as a result, the idea of a shotgun approach to reach a wide market doesn't make sense.

In his book *The Self-Publishing Manual*, author Dan Poynter observes that, "A one-half page ad in a national book-oriented magazine might run you $1,850. Using round numbers and assuming you printed the book for $2 and are selling it for $20, you would have to sell 102 books at retail, or 308 books at wholesale, just to break even on the ad. Experience tells us that you will be lucky to get five orders."

Additionally, it is almost impossible to see the effect of advertising. People don't really seem to buy books in response to ads, but sometimes ads serve to remind them if they have already heard about the book from someone or some other source.

Another reason that publishers hesitate to spend money advertising is that publishers know the greatest publicity for a new book is free, and given in the form of reviews, articles, features, and appearances on national television and radio shows. Think about the $1,850 figure that Dan Poynter used. How many review copies could be sent for that amount of money? How many press releases? How many press kits could be assembled and sent to interested reviewers or producers of television and radio shows?

Publicity Versus Advertising

Publicity is relatively free of cost; advertising is not. But on the other hand, advertising gives you a great deal more control over communicating your message than does publicity. With those caveats in mind, advertising may have a place in the promotion of your book. Authors have successfully used advertising approaches in the form of direct mail, telemarketing, magazine advertising, newspaper advertising, radio/TV commercials, Internet advertising, and placing ads in trade and professional journals.

If you are thinking about advertising, we believe that there are three major considerations when deciding whether or not to advertise your book:

1. **Look at costs very carefully.** Investigate how to get the most advertising for your money. For example, if you have written a romance novel, *Romantic Times* magazine offers discounted rates to authors for a variety of advertising and services. A one-half page, four-color ad space in their magazine (circulation over 135,000) costs $1,000; the same size black-and-white ad space costs $475. On the other hand, if you would like to distribute

your flyers, bookmarks, or other promotional literature to their distributor network or to their network of bookstores that support romantic fiction, it can be done quite affordably, usually from $100 to $300. You can contact *Romantic Times* by calling (718) 237-1097, or going to their Web site at *www.romantictimes.com.* After you have calculated your advertising costs, you are in a better position to consider if these same dollars might be better spent in generating publicity.

2. **Target, Target, Target.** It is imperative that you understand your target market and use your advertising dollars in the most effective way possible. You want to reach those people who demonstrate the greatest probability of reading your book. For example, if you are going to use direct mail to reach your potential readers, you should try to buy a mailing list that absolutely includes those people—and only those people—who will be interested in your book. The same goes for placing advertising in print or electronic media. Advertising is simply too expensive to waste. It is critical that you make a direct hit on the appropriate target market.

3. **You have to make it snap, crackle, and pop!** There is both an art and science to writing good ads, direct mail, or commercial copy. It is critical that you know the basics of effective advertising. If not, then hire someone who does, but consider that cost also.

Advertising Options

A few thoughts about direct mail are worth mentioning, since this MAY represent a relatively low-cost, effective way to target market your book. If you DO decide to use direct mail advertising, you can target the appropriate market by buying mailing lists from mailing list brokers. The current *Literary Market Place* lists more than eighty-eight of these brokers. Some of these mailing list brokers deal with specific target areas. For example, if you have written a scholarly book or a book on how to study effectively, you might want to contact CMG Information Services (*www.cmgdirect.com*), a company that has lists of more than 690,000 college professors, continuing education coordinators, and librarians. On the other hand, if you have written a book about baby boomers or a book that is set in a specific location, you should probably contact Harte-Hanks Direct Marketing (*www.dmamail.com*), a firm that has national resident lists and demographic selectivity. And that medical murder mystery can always be targeted by Reed Reference (phone: 800-521-8110), a broker that has mailing lists reaching more than 380,000 board-certified physicians.

An alternative direct mailing choice is to go with a full-service mailing list broker who can zero in on almost any target. These general, full-service mailing list brokers will help you identify your target audience, recommend appropriate lists, get the best rental terms for the lists, analyze the results, and help with follow-up planning. Some companies even offer promotional copy writing and graphic design. Three of these firms are:

Leon Henry Inc.
455 Central Avenue
Scarsdale, NY 10583
Phone: (914) 723-3176
Web site: *www.leonhenryinc.com*

Fairfield Marketing Group, Inc.
830 Sport Hill Road
Easton, CT 06612-1250
Phone: (203) 261-0885
Web site: *www.ed-pak.com/fairfield/fairprin.html*

ADC Direct Marketing Services Inc.
266 Mobile, Suite 205
Camarillo, CA 93010
Phone: (805) 987-3466
Web site: *www.alandrey.com*

Hiring a Public Relations Firm

If you have decided that you indeed want to hire an advertising or public relations firm, you need to be sure that you will be getting the most for your money. A good, full-service firm should offer the following basic services: media advertising, sales promotion, national publicity, media buying, media kit production, market research, author tours, and Internet marketing. The *Literary Market Place* lists sixty-nine advertising agencies and 137 public relations firms that target the book industry. If you decide to hire a firm, it is well worth your while to read through these listings to see the different types of services offered. You can also find this information on their Web site: *www.literarymarketplace.com*. Here are three advertising/promotional firms that not only offer full service but also offer a little bit extra, as we've noted:

About Books Inc.
P.O. Box 1500-PR
Buena Vista, CA 81211
Phone: (719) 395-2459
Web site: *www.about-books.com*
*Includes direct mailing

Weis Public Relations
2828 Seventh Street
Berkeley, CA 94710
Phone: (510) 841-9347
E-mail: *weispr@lanminds.com*
*Author development, conference organization

Blitz Media-Direct
7 Putter Land
Middle Island, NY 11953-0102
Phone: (613) 924-8555
*Sunday supplements, trade shows

There are plenty of good books about advertising, direct mail, and the like. If you choose to advertise, we highly recommend that you start by reading Chapter 10 in John Kremer's book *1001 Ways to Market Your Book*. This is an excellent resource. It is worth reading the whole thing and can be obtained at most bookstores or by writing, faxing, or calling the publisher:

Open Horizons
P.O. Box 205
Fairfield, IA 52556-0205
Phone: (641) 472-6130 or (800) 796-6130
Fax: (641) 472-1560

Even if you are not self-publishing, Dan Poynter's book *The Self-Publishing Manual* (ninth edition) contains excellent chapters on book promotion. Look in your local bookstore or order it by writing or calling:

Para Publishing
530 Ellwood Ridge Road
Santa Barbara, CA 93117-1047
Phone: (805) 968-7277
Fax: (805) 968-1379
Web site: *www.parapublishing.com*

Advertising on the Internet

Advertising on the Internet is another option. Large commercial Web sites usually offer opportunities for you to get your book noticed. Writers Write, a Web site dedicated to writers and the publishing industry, offers banners and sponsorship buttons that rotate across their extensive network of Web pages. For current rates, visit their site at *www.writerswrite.com/advertising*. This should give you an idea of what you might have to budget if you want to advertise on the World Wide Web.

If you do decide to advertise on the Internet, be sure you ask the right questions. Check to see how many hits the site gets per week and how many links it has. Contact one or two advertisers to see how satisfied they are with the service.

Two books that should help you with your online advertising are:

The Complete Idiot's Guide to Online Marketing, by Bill Eager and Cathy McCall. Que, 1999.

Advertising on the Internet, 2nd Edition, by Robbin Lee Zeff and Brad Aronson. John Wiley & Sons, 1999.

Points to Remember

- The publishing industry balks at spending money advertising new books.
- Books are considered a "low ticket" item with a small profit margin.
- The best publicity for a new book is free.
- Publicity is relatively free of cost; advertising is not.
- Advertising gives you more control over your message than publicity.
- Investigate how to get the most advertising for your money.
- Compare advertising costs versus dollars for publicity.
- With direct mail, targeting with specific mailing lists is the key to success.
- When choosing an advertising agency, carefully research services offered.

5

The Book Signing

Now is the time we call "the agony and the ecstasy." You are delighted because your book is finally in the stores, but you are afraid that people will read it and not like it. What's more, now you have to talk to the readers who HAVE read it! It's hard to smile when your mouth is dry. So put Vaseline on your teeth and get a move on. Hey, beauty queens do it—and for good reason. They want to present a confident image so the judges will like them and vote for them. In your case, you want your judges to like you and buy your book.

OK, maybe you can skip the Vaseline but being prepared is what will do the trick for you! Pick up your pen and take notes while we investigate the world of "the book signing."

It has been our experience that, unless you have written an indefensible and controversial book, booksellers are very happy to have you visit their store for a book signing. These events are good business for the bookstores and can be good business for you. Book signings can be fun, interesting, and you may even sell a few books to people browsing around the store. So, no reason to delay! Let's take a look at how to set up a successful book signing.

Before the Book Signing

One of the most important first steps you can take in arranging a book signing is contacting your publisher. Coordination of effort is critical, and you don't want to step all over any plans your publisher may have already made. What if you had a signing and two weeks later the publisher sent you really cool posters you could have used to advertise the event? That happened to Karen. She couldn't believe the great posters that arrived in the mail three days after her first signing. You'd better believe she called her publisher before she made her next move!

Your publisher can also help you take advantage of any contacts he has with the bookstore, either telling you the right approach to take or calling the manager himself. Coordination with your publisher is also critical when it comes to making sure your books will arrive at the bookstore on time. Yes, everyone has agreed to the signing, but ultimately it is the author who has to make sure the books are there to be signed.

The Initial Contact

You're excited. Your book is on the shelves, and you want to go full steam ahead with your first signing. You have every right to be excited! Now take a deep breath and relax, because you're about to make your sales pitch. Asking a bookstore to participate in a signing is exactly that. The proper approach is important.

Remember what we have said before about approaching bookstores. Try to find a local author who has recently had a book signing at the store and call for advice and information. Your first contact with the store should be by phone to make a simple inquiry to see if the store is interested in a signing. If the manager or community relations coordinator says they don't want to participate in a signing, simply leave your name and number in case they change their mind. You should NOT walk in and *expect* to have a chat with the manager or anyone else. These are busy folks, and no one likes to be caught unprepared. Give them a call and tell them you'd like to come by to talk about arranging a signing. Set up a meeting. This will give them time to get their ducks in a row.

When you are preparing for the meeting, be aware that, just as your book was judged before the store decided to sell it, you will be judged as someone the store may or may not want sitting at their entrance talking with customers. To that end, be well groomed and personable. Try not to overwhelm the manager with your ideas. Read through this section a few times and make a list of questions to take with you so you have your facts straight about times, date, book ordering responsibility, and promotion.

When planning a date for your book signing, keep in mind that most signings usually last about two hours and most bookstores like to hold their signings on weekends during the day or weeknights in the early evening. Bookstores located in malls seem to prefer 1:00 to 3:00 P.M. on Saturday afternoons, which is when customer traffic is heaviest.

You will want to make your initial contact with the bookseller at least six weeks in advance of your proposed book signing date. Bookstores need that amount of time to both order your book and promote your book signing. Some booksellers do an excellent job of promoting their book signings, while others seem to leave the turnout up to fate. The booksellers who are adept at promotion will need all the advance notice you can give them in order to effectively promote your book signing. They will use this extra time to include your book-signing date in their newsletters, to place the date in the calendar of the local newspaper, and to prepare flyers and signs to arrange in their store to let customers know about your upcoming visit.

Some of the more aggressive booksellers will even run small ads in the local newspaper a few days before your appearance. When you first approach your bookseller, be sure to ask what plans they have to promote your signing. The larger stores, such as Barnes & Noble, will do everything we've described. Barnes & Noble even produces their own beautiful, professional posters that they give to the authors as a memento.

It has been our experience that most bookstores are happy to participate in a signing, even the large, somewhat formidable chains. Several bookstore managers have told us that signings are not only good for the store but are also good for the manager, who appears involved with the reading community. We have had to shuffle our schedules, pitch in and help get our books to the store on time, and even do some of our own promotion, but we've never had a store refuse a signing. A call to the two major chain stores in our area revealed that only a very small percentage of signings were refused and that those refusals were mostly due to problems the bookstore had getting books from the publisher/distributor. One store refused a signing because of the highly controversial nature of the book itself. So unless you've written a book about the sex lives of transvestites and are trying to arrange a signing in the Bible Belt, we think you have an excellent chance of arranging a signing with almost any bookstore.

Other bookstores may not have the staff or the budget to do much promotion. If this is the case, you will have to place notices in the newspapers and post flyers yourself. Remember to call the local television and radio stations and ask that your book signing be included in their community calendars.

It has been our experience that small, independent booksellers are often particularly willing to extend themselves by heavily promoting a book signing for an author in whom they are interested. In spite of a bookstore's best efforts, however, book signings, though fun, are not usually very productive in terms of book sales unless you engage in collateral publicity locally. By collateral publicity we mean television, radio, newspaper, and magazine coverage. We will explain how to publicize your book signing using the media in Chapter 7.

The Follow-up

If your book signing is being held at a local bookstore, try to stop by two weeks before the date to see how things are going. If it is scheduled to take place out of town, it is critical that you call the bookstore at this time to confirm the date. That way you won't arrive in Cleveland, walk in the bookstore, and have them say, "What? We thought your signing was next month!"

Regardless, your contact with the bookseller two weeks ahead of time serves as both a reminder and an opportunity to solve problems before they arise. Talk with the manager or the person assigned to organizing and running the book signing. Ask how many books they have, or will have, on hand. They should have at least fifty or more. They are better off having too many than too few. They can always return them to the publisher or distributor if necessary (unless you sign them—then generally, the bookseller has to keep them no matter if they sell or not!). This is also the time to give the bookseller any promotional material that you may have, including:

- Flyers
- Publicity photo
- Press kit
- Bookmarks
- Posters

If your publisher has not printed any posters for your book and the bookstore doesn't have the budget to make their own, make one yourself. Go to your local photocopy shop and have your book cover enlarged to poster size. Have them paste it to a stiff cardboard-type backing. The bookstore can use your poster for publicity during the week before your signing, and it can be placed at the entrance the day you are there. Your poster should be as eye-catching as possible. Make sure it includes an author photo and a book cover.

The Day of the Signing

It's here and you can't wait—to either run to the bookstore or hide under the bed. Remember, that which does not kill us makes us strong! Most fears can be subdued by taking a hands-on approach. That means make a list so you don't forget anything! Here is ours:

Things to Take to Your Book Signing

Make sure you bring cool pens—and ones that write! Fountain pens are very hip, but the ink takes awhile to dry and can be quite messy. Also be sure to bring your business cards and bookmarks.

You should also bring something to read or work on during lulls. Sitting and twiddling your thumbs both looks and feels awkward. Editing a current first draft or making notes for the next great American novel will help you feel more at ease. Also, people are fascinated with the writing process and may stop just to see what you are working on. That's an opportunity to sell yourself and your book!

It's also a good idea to bring breath mints. Your throat may become dry as you talk with people, and you don't want to be remembered as "that nice author with the overpowering bad breath."

This might sound like unnecessary advice, but you should also make sure you have clean hands. Your hands will be on display, and your nails should be clean and well groomed.

Don't forget your best manners! Remember, you are not only selling your book, you are selling yourself as an author. You will be dealing with the general public, and they can make thoughtless and sometimes cruel remarks. Don't take it personally. Some people don't realize what they are saying, and others will be a bit jealous. Karen had to listen to quite a few people tell her that anyone could write a romance novel, while others told her they knew that romance writers just used the same plot over and over, only changing the names. Karen just smiled (and made simply awful replies under her breath). You should try to do that too (just the smiling part). After all, these are the people who will be telling their friends about you and your book.

Remember to wear comfortable but professional clothing. No, you don't have to dress like a corporate drone unless your book is about succeeding in the business world. You can wear a frilly dress if you are a romance writer, or black leather if you are writing about a motorcycle road trip. It really doesn't matter. Just be sure your outfit looks good, doesn't show sweat, and has a loose waistband (remember, you will be sitting for at least two hours).

Signings sometimes involve the author reading a selection from his book. It's a good idea to pick an excerpt from your book beforehand, choosing one that is both lively and intriguing. Your goal is to make the listeners want to know more and thus buy your book! Karen chose a selection from *Kingdom of Hearts* where the heroine meets the king by tumbling through a secret curtained alcove and landing on his bedroom floor. She stopped the reading at the point where the king approaches the curtain-wrapped form, notices that the bundle has a nicely shaped posterior and gently nudges said posterior with his toe. Needless to say, the listeners wanted to know more! Once you select your excerpt, practice reading it out loud several times, preferably in front of family or friends.

What to Do When You Get There

Be sure to arrive at least 15 minutes early to catch your breath, relax, and get the feel of the situation. You should allow time to check out where the store has you located and make changes in that location if necessary. Experienced managers already know where to place you. You should be in a high-traffic area near the front of the store. Readers should have to pass your table to get into and out of the bookstore. If the manager is inexperienced and has placed you near the back of the store, use your best manners and ask to be placed in the front. If you are in a mall, ask the manager to have the mall announce that you are there for your book signing.

You should have a table with a chair and multiple copies of your books nicely arranged. The manager will often offer you a glass of water or a soft drink, and you should take it. If they do not offer it, ask for a glass of water even if you aren't thirsty at the time. Hopefully, your mouth will dry up from your conversations with your legions of fans who have formed a serpentine queue around the store.

Once you are all set, visit the bathroom for one last pit stop and to make sure your face is clean. Now you are ready to take the walk down that runway!

How to Win the Pageant

Make no mistake about it: you will be on stage. What else would you call sitting in the front of a store behind a table with your books piled around you? Your demeanor can either make people want to approach you and talk about your book, or it can drive them away. So sit up straight and keep a pleasant smile on your face. Watch people as they walk by—you know, casually, like you do book signings all of the time. When someone meets your eye, give them a smile. Six out of ten people will come over to see why you are sitting there. They will ask relatively dumb questions, such as, "Did you write this book?" They will ask thoughtful questions, such as, "How long did it take to write the book?" And they will surprise you with some of their observations.

Be sure you have plenty of books on the table for the readers to pick up. People who read books like to touch them, turn them over, thumb through the pages. Offer to answer any questions, make comments about how much fun it was to write the book, be excited. Being assertive like this can be quite difficult for some people, especially introverted writers, but you simply must extend yourself and make contact with each potential reader. If someone has the chance to meet you, talk with you, and feel your book in their hands, they are more likely to buy your book.

That's what this book signing is all about. These people are giving you a wonderful gift—interest in the fruits of your creative effort. Respect them and write something nice in their book when they buy a copy.

This brings us to the issue of what to say when you sign your book for strangers.

You should plan this in advance. It doesn't have to be lengthy and may consist only of your signature and the date. Karen often wrote "Enjoy!" then added her name and the date. If you have a minute to chat with your book buyer, don't hesitate to include something personal if it seems appropriate. For example, a woman approached Kathleen during her book signing at Barnes & Noble for *Awakening at Midlife*. She said she was buying the book as a birthday gift and asked Kathleen to sign it for her good friend who was turning fifty. In addition to her normal book message, Kathleen added, "Happy 50th Birthday." Ten minutes later, this woman reappeared with three more copies of the book in her hands. She had read the personal message, liked it, and before she left the store thought about three other friends who were having midlife birthdays.

Very important note: DON'T ever assume that you know how to spell someone's name, even simple names that you think you know. You don't want to mar the book by scratching through your misspelled salutation. Always ask, "Is that 'Carol' spelled C-A-R-O-L?" Often the reader will say, "No, it has an 'e' on the end." Or, "No, it's Carroll." Rule of thumb: You can add an 'e' to Carol, but you can't take one away without looking like a goof. At large book signings for famous authors who draw hundreds of fans, each person is usually given an index card or a small piece of paper on which to clearly print the name they would like written in the book. Until you get to that point, make sure you know how to spell the person's name by asking. Also, always sign on the title page, not the first blank page. When you are a famous writer, your autographed copy will be worth a great deal more when it is signed on the page that includes your title and publisher.

And remember, you need to win the pageant with the bookstore too. *Be helpful and polite with the staff.* Karen made sure her book signing in Hampton, Virginia, went smoothly. The staff at Waldenbooks thought she was so easy to work with and so funny with the customers that they invited her to come back and sign books on the cherished "day after Thanksgiving" shopping marathon! Karen cajoled over 150 people to buy her book that day.

What to Do after the Signing

Before you leave the bookstore, graciously offer to autograph as many of your books as they want. Many bookstore managers will ask you to do this anyway. Remember what we said earlier: signed books usually cannot be returned to the publisher, and you'll receive the royalties from those books! Also, be sure to send a thank-you note to the bookstore. You never know when your next book will come out. As an especially nice gesture, if a bookstore manager has knocked himself out helping to make your book signing a roaring success, why not drop a nice note to his regional manager? As we like to say, "What goes around, comes around." And one last thing: be sure to stop by the bookstore two weeks after your signing. This gives you a chance to reinforce the contact, and, as Karen found, if they've run out of signed copies, you can graciously sign new ones, too!

Alternative Book Signings

Keep in mind that bookstores aren't the only places where you can hold book signings. Your book can have very good sales at other locations if you have accurately targeted your market.

Where to Look

Let's say you have written a cookbook. In that case, an appearance at Williams & Sonoma could be very productive. If you have written a book about a young girl's friendship with her pony, hold a book signing at a store that sells riding equipment. What about a book signing at your old high school or college? Remember the author's questionnaire we talked about? Take another look at it, and target as many alternate places for book signings as you can.

You should also check newspapers for fairs, carnivals, and other gatherings. The book about the young girl and her pony would sell nicely at a horse show. Approach the organizers and ask if you can set up a table. Be sure to give yourself plenty of time for the distributor to ship the books to you or for the store to receive them from the publisher, distributor, or wholesaler.

Alternative book-signing opportunities are everywhere! For Karen's novel *Kingdom of Hearts*, she has sold books at a women's fair, a garden center opening, and an art show. She even sold multiple copies of her book at a military air show, where she encouraged the men in the audience to buy copies of the book for their wives or girlfriends. She told each man that the novel had several racy scenes in it, and if his wife read it, he might get lucky. Guess what? Every man who heard that pitch bought a copy of the book!

Things to Keep in Mind

The important thing to remember about these non-bookstore signings is that your involvement is going to be critical. The management and staff at these locations are probably not experienced in running successful book signings. If you are arranging such a book signing, look back through the entire "book signing" section and make a list of everything the bookstore is supposed to do and add it to your own list of things to do.

Another important thing to remember about non-bookstore signings is that you will be the one supplying the books, and that means purchasing them from your publisher. Most publishing contracts state the author discount, which is usually 40 percent. (In some cases, you may also receive royalties for these books even though you purchased them, but most often you will not.) Talk to your publisher. Try to get a bigger discount. One way to do this is by offering to buy large quantities of your book, say 300 to 500 copies. If that doesn't get the discount lowered, offer to make the books nonreturnable. Publishers love that, and the extra 10- or 20-percent discount can only be to your benefit. As for having an extra hundred or so books on hand, believe us when we say you'll be glad you did, especially when the Rotary Club calls at the last minute inviting you to give a speech!

Another option for purchasing your book is to do so through your local bookstore. You will have to negotiate with them about the discount you will receive, and it will be less than what you will get from the publisher. If you do decide to go through the bookstore, offer to have a sign on your table saying that the book can also be purchased at their store. That should help with the negotiations and smooth any ruffled feathers about a "non-bookstore signing."

Private Book Signings

You may also want to explore the idea of holding a private signing reception sponsored by good friends. For example, two of Kathleen's closest friends felt that they knew lots of people who would be interested in buying and reading her book. One friend works for a major mental health organization, and the other is a spiritual director at an Episcopal church. Since Kathleen's book, *Awakening at Midlife*, presents both a psychological and spiritual approach to midlife, their combined list of personal contacts was an excellent target market for her book. They issued the invitations about a month in advance, inviting people to join them in celebrating their friend's new book. The invitations let people know they would have a chance to meet the author, purchase a book, and have it signed if they wished. Kathleen's friends set up a beautiful gathering at their home with wine, cheese, and other goodies. Kathleen arranged for the manager of a local Waldenbooks to order books ahead of time from her publisher, Riverhead Books, as well as handle sales on the night of the reception. Needless to say, the private book signing was a great success. Kathleen signed (and sold!) more than 100 books that night.

Book signings, for most authors, are great fun. Finding locations to sell and sign your book is limited only by your creativity and your firm understanding of your target market—those who will buy your book.

Many books become successful by word of mouth. Some even hit the local bestseller list this way. But as we said earlier, it is critical that your book signing—indeed, all of your book promotions—is supported by publicity. The more people who know about your book, the better your sales will be. In this day and age, the best way to spread the word is through the electronic and print media, which we will discuss in Chapter 7.

Points to Remember

- Book signings are good business for the bookstores and for you.
- Make initial contact with the bookseller at least six weeks in advance of your proposed books-signing date.
- Ask what plans they have to promote your book signing.
- Follow up two weeks before your book signing.
- Have a checklist for the day of the signing.
- Remember that your demeanor can either attract or repel potential book buyers.
- Plan ahead what you will write in the books that you will sign.
- Offer to autograph any or all of the books left over from the signing.
- Be sure to send a thank-you note to the bookstore.
- Target as many alternative places for book signings as you can.
- Keep at least fifty books on hand for last-minute signings.
- Hold a private book signing hosted by friends.

6

The Book Tour

A well planned book tour is an important part of making your book a success. Publishers routinely send their major authors on tours to big cities throughout the country. These publishers have full-time publicity staffs who make sure that their authors receive good coverage in each city they visit. Radio and television interviews are arranged, and reviews and newspaper feature articles coincide with book signings and other public events. Big-time authors have nothing more to do than get to the airport on time and be shuttled to this interview or that book signing. Although this type of schedule can be quite a handful for an author who does not have the advantage of a publicist or the resources of a major publishing house, we have some ideas that can help.

Reality Based Options

If you don't have a publicist, you have two options: (1) hire a promotional firm or an independent publicist; or (2) do it yourself. Let's take a look.

Hiring Outside Promotion

If you decide to hire a promotional firm or an independent publicist, choose one that specializes in arranging and managing book tours and other aspects of book marketing. Many advertise in *Publishers Weekly* and other industry magazines. We suggest that you carefully scrutinize such businesses. As in all of life, you will find the good, the bad, and the ugly among them. The good ones—and there are many excellent companies—represent authors' next best chance for success if their publishers do not publicize their books and if they can't personally spend a lot of time doing so. These companies can do all or part of any campaign: pitch books to national shows, set up radio interviews, or organize an entire author tour.

Know that most of these services are expensive and these companies work months in advance. If you are interested in pursuing this option, call several and ask for a complete set of rates and note whether you have to pay for each contact made on your behalf or just the shows you appear on. Ask for a copy of a recent tour schedule, one that was developed for a book similar to yours. Also ask for a list of authors whom the firm has represented, and contact these authors to see if they are satisfied. It is also a good idea to call one or two of the radio or television stations the company targets and ask their opinion of the promotional firm. It's your money, and you can't be too careful!

An extensive listing of these types of companies can also be found in the *Literary Market Place*. We suggest that you take the time to read these listings and note which companies emphasize author tours. To get you started, here are three that we like:

Accent on Broadcasting Etc., Inc.
165 West 66th Street, Suite 16-G
New York, NY 10023
Phone: (212) 362-3616

Brody Public Relations
145 Rt. 519
Stockton, NJ 08559-1711
Phone: (609) 397-3737
E-mail: *rbbb@voicenet.com*
Planned Television Arts

Richard Frishman
1110 2nd Avenue, 3rd floor
New York, NY 10022
Phone: (212) 593-5820
E-mail: *frishmanr@ruderfinn.com*

Arranging Your Own Tour

The second option, and a good one if you are on a limited budget, is to arrange your own book tour. It is not impossible to do, and it is an important part of getting the word out about your book. Yes, it is challenging, and yes, it will take up quite a bit of your time, but by arranging your own book tour you can take advantage of your creativity and design a tour package that suits both your aspirations and your budget.

Arranging your own book tour is a matter of making sure that you have good media coverage in every city you visit. It is critical that you build synergy and support between local media and bookstore events or talks about your book (or subject). In this section we will show you the steps you need to take in order to coordinate radio and television interviews, newspaper feature articles, and local events so they coincide with your signings.

It is important that you let your publisher know beforehand about your plans for a book tour. Coordination in this area is crucial. Your publisher may have plans of his own for sending you on the road. If that's not the case, your publisher can certainly help you with information about good book markets, tell you what has worked on other author tours, and maybe even supply you with flyers. During the past several years, Kathleen has developed a robust speaking program and travels around the country giving talks and workshops. Her publisher is always the first to know when she schedules a talk in a particular city and has been very successful in getting media attention in those places. Publishers have good contacts with bookstore managers and are pretty savvy about the media, so you want to take advantage of any advice they can give.

A word about this section. What we are doing is giving you a step-by-step plan of attack. Most of these steps overlap with information elsewhere in the book. In this section we will tell you *what to do* and then refer you to the section that goes into great detail about *how to do it*.

Step 1: Select Your City

There are two considerations when choosing where you might travel for your book signing: (1) cost; and (2) market size. If you are on a tight budget, select a city relatively close to your home to keep travel expenses to a minimum. You can choose cities farther afield if you have really great friends living there who would love for you to stay with them. (In particular, choose great friends with nice homes, who are gourmet cooks, and who keep their wine cellar well stocked. A swimming pool is nice, but optional. Remember, this is a business trip.) Transportation and lodging costs can add up very quickly.

If you decide to travel by air, remember that the cost of airline tickets fluctuates wildly. To get the best fares, make reservations at least twenty-one days in advance, and plan to stay over on a Saturday. Unless you are independently wealthy, be aware of your costs and use every strategy you can think of to keep them to a minimum. Some industry analysts suggest that book tours cost approximately $3,000 per city. That's OK if someone else is paying the overhead, but you can do it for less than that. You must remain highly aware of your costs and remember to keep every single receipt—they can be used as tax deductions once you have made money on your book.

Market size is also important. You might live a mile or two from Monterey, California, which has 13 bookstores, but it's worth the effort to tour San Francisco, which has 144 bookstores. Richmond, Virginia, has 49 bookstores, and if you drive an hour and a half to the east, you can tour the five-city area of Virginia Beach, Norfolk, Hampton, Chesapeake, and Newport News and hit another 111 stores. To find the number of bookstores in each city, turn back to page 60, where we discussed sending flyers to bookstores and using the Internet to determine how many bookstores are in specific markets. Now is the time to cross-reference this information.

Step 2: Bait Your Hook

Once you have targeted your city, you need to find something that makes you interesting to the local media professionals in that area. Think of fishing. To catch a fat bass, first you have to figure out where it lives and then you have to bait an enticing hook. It's the same with the media. Where is their pond (city), and what will make them want to bite and give you that valued interview? A well baited, local hook!

There are two types of well baited local hooks: natural and artificial. (See, just like fishing!) A natural local hook is one that occurs naturally in the area. If you have written a great biography about Grover Cleveland, you know that he was born in Caldwell, New Jersey. So you ask yourself, what major city is located near Caldwell? Can you be there around the date of his birthday, March 18th?

You can also use special dates to promote your book in general. A natural hook that could be used in any city you target could be as simple as a particular date. For example, it was no accident that Bill Cosby's book *Fatherhood* had a publication date just before Father's Day in 1986. Lots of people, hearing about his book, rushed out to buy it for their dads. If you have written a book about space exploration, then surely you know the date and details of John Glenn's second liftoff. That special day would be a logical natural hook for any city you target. Be an unrelenting sleuth for these kinds of tie-ins.

An artificial hook is one you have to make up. We discuss these types of hooks in great detail in Chapter 7, so check out that section for a good list. In the meantime, several examples of artificial hooks include visiting a school or library to conduct a reading, conducting a seminar on your topic, or participating in a charity giveaway by donating a signed copy of your book for an auction.

Public speaking is also a great way to create an artificial hook. We discussed this in Chapter 4, so look back for specific information about how to do this. An added bonus with public speaking is that the group sponsoring your talk can often help generate local publicity and, perhaps, even help absorb some of your travel expenses.

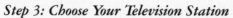

Step 3: Choose Your Television Station

You've chosen the city and baited your hooks. Now it's time to find the best local television station in the area. In Chapter 7, we explain exactly how to go about finding the television station that fits you and your book. For the moment, note that the television station should be the first type of media that you contact. You will get the most exposure on television, so you want to book them first.

Step 4: Choose the Best Show to Promote Your Book

Now that you know which station you are interested in, you need to determine which show on that station is most likely to welcome an interview. Again we go into great detail in Chapter 7 about how to do this. Pay particular attention to the kinds of stories that are generally covered by various programs in your targeted city. Find the right fit. This will save you from wasting your time pitching *101 Advantages of Living Together Instead of Marrying* to a Sunday morning program targeted to fundamentalist Christians.

Step 5: Nail Down the Television Interview

Call your top television station choice about your upcoming visit to their area. If your first contact is not interested, ask nicely for a referral to another reporter or program at the same station that might be interested. Make notes on every conversation. Write reminders for making follow-up calls and mailing material in your day planner. Send materials, return calls, and do your part exactly as you said you would.

Establish a date that you will be available for television interviews. Be sure to choose a date well enough in advance so you will be able to arrange book signings, print interviews, and radio shows to coincide with your appearance on the show.

Step 6: Call the Bookstore

As soon as you have a confirmed date with the television station, call bookstores in the area and tell them you will be in their city for a television show on a certain date and would like to set up a book signing. As we mentioned in Chapter 4, you can find listings of local bookstores by using a good search engine on the Internet. Remember, bookstores need several weeks—or even a month or more—to arrange signings. And don't forget about the independent booksellers. If you have friends who live in the area, ask them which of the independents are the best. Try to have at least two book signings in the area. If you have time, drop by a few other bookstores in the area to see if they are interested in having you autograph some copies of your books even if you can't participate in a book signing. You don't have to call ahead; showing up is fine and less complicated on a tight schedule.

Step 7: Get into the Print Media

Now that your television and book-signing dates are set, find out about all the print media (e.g., newspapers, local magazines, etc.) in your target city. Again, make a list, and be sure to note the lead times each periodical needs to get the advertisements or feature articles published. Here is where you will really begin to appreciate your large wall calendar!

Call the newspapers and local magazines to tell them you will be in their city for several book signings. Let them know that you're scheduled to be on certain television shows on their local network affiliate. They should be happy to do a feature on you. Newspaper interviews can be conducted over the phone, although most reporters would prefer to meet you in person. That gives them the opportunity to take photographs—an especially important part of a feature article. However, if this cannot be accomplished because of time demands, travel considerations, and so forth, tell the reporter that you will immediately send a copy of your book and your press kit—which contains a black-and-white photo of you and, in the best circumstances, a color photo of your book cover. This should give the reporter two graphic elements that can be included in your story. If you do meet the reporter face-to-face, bring an extra press kit and copy of your book. Finally, include a cover letter that thanks the paper for their interest and reiterates the details of when you will be conducting your television interview and book signings.

Step 8: Contact Radio Shows

You should now call the local radio shows. Tell them about your book tour, including the television shows you will be on and the book signings. See if you can get on one of their shows. Take a look at Chapter 7, which gives explicit details on how to pitch to a radio producer. It's possible to do a radio interview several days in advance by telephone, so keep that option in mind.

Step 9: Announce Your Tour on the Internet

Now that everything is set up, it is time to announce the tour on the Internet. There are several good sites that list author tours. The Bookwire site (*www.bookwire.com*) is listed on NetGuide's "Ultimate Hotlist: The 50 Best Places to Go Online," and it will include your free listing in its *Publishers Weekly* guide to "Authors on the Highway." This is a great place to spread the word about your tour. Other sites, especially those dedicated to writers, will carry information about your tour as well.

Be sure to let the online bookstores that sell your book know about your tour. Also contact any news groups, Web rings, and writers groups you participate in. Ask if you can have their e-mail list so you can send electronic flyers. And be sure that your tour is posted on your Web site.

A Book Tour Example

The secret to setting up a book tour lies in coordination, perseverance, and follow-up. As we stated earlier, attracting local media interest is not difficult as long as you have a hook that piques the interest of the people living in that locale. Establishing a book tour requires only that you target particular locations and follow through by setting up media exposure and book signings. It can be done. Kathleen's visit to Roanoke, Virginia, is a great example.

The PBS program "The Midlife Survival Guide," which was based on Kathleen's book, was scheduled to air throughout the country during the spring of 1997. Kathleen had lived in Roanoke, Virginia, for more than ten years, and as an independent producer, she had worked with WBRA, the PBS station in Roanoke, on certain specials. That same spring she received a telephone call from WBRA, asking her to be an on-air personality for their Spring Fund-Raiser (affectionately known as the "Beg-A-Thon"). She had a natural local hook, and as soon as she confirmed her appearance on WBRA, she made calls to other local media and bookstores. As a result of her efforts, she conducted two book signings, had an on-air appearance on PBS, and was the subject of an excellent local feature in the newspaper during her brief visit there. The newspaper reporter proved to be very helpful and arranged to run the article about Kathleen in the local paper just a few days before her visit. In addition, WBRA ran their own ad about the television special that also appeared in the local newspaper.

Now, admittedly, this was Roanoke, Virginia, and not New York City, but both of Kathleen's book signings were mobbed.

One of the bookstores even ran out of books to sell, and Kathleen has been told that Roanoke continues to sell a great many of her books! As you can see, even though she was only in the city for a weekend, she accomplished a great deal in promoting her book.

You might not have the media contacts that Kathleen had, but you certainly have a good book to sell and the determination to make your book tour a success. Take a look back through this section and start sketching out a plan. Access the Internet sites we told you about and see which markets can give you the most bang for the buck. And remember, don't be afraid to call those television stations, radio producers, and newspaper columnists. You have a good product that can help increase their audience base. Confidence is a good thing! Appendix B details some of Kathleen's book tour material.

Points to Remember

- Local hooks are critical when targeting a city for a book tour.
- Keep travel expenses to a minimum by targeting nearby cities.
- Keep all receipts for tax deductions.
- Choose a date well enough in advance to coordinate all appearances, noting advance time for book shipments and lead time for print mediums.
- Target every major television and radio station and newspaper in your chosen cities.

7

The Media

It's everywhere. Like death and taxes, you simply can't avoid it. What are we talking about? The media, of course! It invades almost every aspect of our lives. The radio is on in the car; the television is on in several rooms of the house; when you grab a quick bite to eat, a magazine is usually in your hand; the newspaper shows up at your house every morning. We keep stressing that effective promotion is critical to the success of your book, and nowhere can your promotional effort pay off better than in the media: television, radio, and print. Let's begin with television.

Television: Local Markets

Local markets are not just those cities in which you live. We use the term *local* to mean local to a specific area, generated from that area. You can be in any part of the country doing interviews on local television. Most cities or geographical regions have local affiliates of ABC, CBS, NBC, FOX, UPN, and PBS.

Choosing a Local Market

As you decide where you want to promote your book on local television, the first thing you should do is choose that local market carefully. Be practical in terms of travel and expenses, and reasonable in terms of geography. If you are writing about the New York mayoral race, a market covering rural Pennsylvania or Ohio is not what you're looking for. Next, choose a market that reaches a large number of viewers. The more viewers a local TV market has, the more people you will be able to reach with the news of your wonderful new book. For a listing of Nielsen-rated markets, which gives the number of households in that market, you can go to *www.newsblues.com*. For example, the largest market in the country as of January 2000 was the New York City metropolitan area, which has 6,874,990 households. Then again, North Platte came in as Market Number 209, with only 14,550 households, so pick your market carefully. Additional geographic and population density information can be found by taking a look at a television market's *Area of Dominant Influence* (or, as it is known in the business, ADI). The ADI is a map that shows the geographic area that the local market's television stations cover and the number of people living in those areas. You can get an ADI by calling the sales department of one of the television stations in a particular market. To access a complete listing of markets by region, go to *http://dir.yahoo.com/News_and_Media/Television/By_Region/*.

It's easy to find markets that have plenty of television opportunities. For example, Denver has the three affiliates (ABC, CBS, and NBC), plus PBS, FOX, and a regional cable channel. In

Seattle there are eleven stations, including the networks plus public access, arts, news, and community information stations.

Again, remember that local television markets are not just those in which you live but are those generated from that area. You can indeed be in any part of the country doing interviews on local television. Once you've happily done interviews in your home-town, you might consider spreading your wings. For the confident and ambitious, here is a list of the top give local television markets in the country. That which does not kill us makes us strong!

NEW YORK:

ABC-WABC
7 Lincoln Square Plaza
New York, NY 10023
Phone (212) 456-4177

NBC-WNBC
News Center 4
30 Rockefeller Center, #701
New York, NY 10018
Phone: (212) 664-4444

CBS-WCBS
51 West 52nd Street
New York, NY 10019
Phone: (212) 975-4321

PBS-WNET
450 West 33rd Street
New York, NY 10001
Phone: (212) 560-1313

LOS ANGELES:

ABC-KABC
4151 Prospect Avenue
Hollywood, CA 90027
Phone: (323) 644-7777

CBS-KCBS
6121 West Sunset Boulevard
Hollywood, CA 90028
Phone: (323) 460-3000

NBC-KNBC
3000 West Alameda Avenue
Burbank, CA 91532
Phone: (818) 840-4444

PBS-KCET
4401 Sunset Boulevard
Los Angeles, CA 90027
Phone: (323) 666-5600

CHICAGO:

ABC-WLS
190 North State Street #800
Chicago, IL 60601
Phone: (312) 984-0890

CBS-WBBM
630 North McClurg Court
Chicago, IL 60611
Phone: (312) 951-3497

NBC-WMAQ
455 North Cityfront Plaza
Drive
Chicago, IL 60611
Phone: (312) 245-6120

PBS-WTTW
5440 North St. Louis Avenue
Chicago, IL 60625
Phone: (773) 509-1111

PHILADELPHIA:

ABC-WPVI
4100 City Line Avenue
Philadelphia, PA 19106
Phone: (215) 878-9700

CBS-WKYW
101 South Independence
Mall East
Philadelphia, PA 19131
Phone: (215) 238-4700

NBC-WCAU
10 Monument Road
Bala Cynwyd, PA 19004
Phone: (610) 668-5510

PBS-WHYY
150 North 6th Street
Philadelphia, PA 19106
Phone: (215) 351-1200

SAN FRANCISCO:

ABC-KGO
900 Front Street
San Francisco, CA 94111
Phone: (415) 478-3810

CBS-KPIX
855 Battery Street
San Francisco, CA 94111
Phone: (415) 362-5550

NBC-KRON
1001 Van Ness Avenue
San Francisco, CA 94109
Phone: (415) 441-4444

PBS-KQED
2601 Mariposa Street
San Francisco, CA 94110
Phone: (415) 553-2129

A complete television station listing guide will cost you $50, so you might want to share the cost with several other authors. To purchase one, contact NATPE International (*www.natpe.com*).

Choosing a Local Television Station

Once you have chosen your local market, you will want to see which station has the highest number of viewers for the programs you are interested in. Usually, one station is the leader for all of their news and public affairs shows. This can differ, though, so you want to target the station that has the most viewers for the majority of their shows. Viewership information is given as *ratings* and *shares,* and you will need to know the difference.

Ratings give the percentage of people watching a show out of everyone in the entire viewing area (the ADI). A *share* is the percentage of viewers tuned to a particular newscast or show among people who are actually watching TV at that time. The key here is to pay attention to the *ratings*. This is what the salespeople use to sell advertising, and it is an accurate reflection of how much "bang for the buck" you can get by being on that show or television station. Higher ratings equal more people from the entire area who are watching that show or TV station. *Share* is a tool used by programmers to fine-tune their programs to appeal to the people who are actually watching an individual show. The only time you should pay attention to shares is if the TV stations are in a ratings tie. You should then look at the shares to help you make your decision.

Call the local newspaper and ask for the radio/television columnist. They always have the latest information and should be able to tell you the ratings for both the TV stations and the individual news shows on those stations. Obviously, it is better to target a station that is consistently watched by a higher number of viewers, which is the one with the highest ratings. Be sure to let the columnist know why you are calling. If you catch a columnist in the right mood, you can often receive good inside information. Take care to call when the person has time to speak with you and isn't on a deadline. (Ask the receptionist or secretary when a good time to call might be.) Furthermore, if you are nice enough to the columnist, you just might gain access to the local arts and leisure editor!

Choosing the Show

Your best shot for getting on local TV is to target a morning show. Why? Because most of these shows have live interview segments, and they are hungry for people to interview. After all, not that many folks want to get up at o-dark-thirty and drag out to a TV station to be interviewed. It's hateful when the alarm goes off at 3:00 A.M., but you'll be glad you did it. The exposure is worth it. Your second best bet is the noon news or a locally produced mid-morning show. These also usually have slots for people to be interviewed live. Your chances for landing a morning show spot are almost 90 percent. Your chances of getting a slot on a locally produced mid-morning show are just about as good. As for the noon show, you will be in competition with medium/hard news, but, barring a natural disaster or other sensational event, you have at least a 70-percent shot at getting a guest appearance. These percentages change with the local market you are targeting. Obviously it is more difficult to get a shot on a local morning show in Los Angeles than it is in Richmond, Virginia, but these shows are still your best bet.

How do you approach these shows? Send your press kit to each morning show in your targeted market. Address it to the producer. Be sure to call the station to check on the correct spelling of the producer's name. Nothing is more insulting than receiving a package with your name misspelled! Your cover letter should be brief and to the point, because producers are notoriously busy. Mention a local angle (more on that soon), and offer to participate in an on-air book giveaway. If the show has a call-in segment, tell the producer you will bring five books to give away if the callers can answer simple and silly questions relating to the subject of your book. For example, if you have a romance novel, one question could be, "Who is the romance cover boy who can't believe it's not butter?" (That would be Fabio for those not in the know.) The five books will have to be a write-off; the TV station will not pay for them.

Be sure to mention in your letter that you are available to do both the morning show and an interview segment on the noon show as well. This gives the TV station a chance to cross-promote their shows, which they absolutely love to do!

One week after sending your press kit, make telephone contact. (A brief warning here: never, ever show up uninvited at a TV station and expect anyone to give you the time of day; they are simply too busy.) The best time to phone a morning show producer is 15 minutes after the show goes off the air. Give the producer time to chew out the camera crew, listen to whiny anchors, and go to the bathroom. Realize that morning show producers are usually tired and cranky and have every right to be.

Have your hook ready. Ask if they have received your press kit. Offer to briefly refresh their memory. Be very nice. Present your case, again offering a local angle such as a book signing or a reading at hospital. If you don't have a local angle, offer a gimmick. For example, maybe the anchors could try to guess which on-air personality would make the best leading character.

If the morning show producer gives the thumbs up, explain that you want a "tie-in" with the noon show and that you will call the noon producer yourself. If the morning show producer declines to have you on the show, ask the producer to forward your press kit to the noon producer. Then follow up with a phone call to the noon producer several days later. Just send one press kit—these producers sit beside each other and often share the same desk. The second press kit would be trashed immediately.

Once You Get the Interview

If you do get an interview, watch the show you will be on as many times as you can, even if you have to videotape it. You want to get to know the anchor's interviewing style and sense of humor. You can also pick up pointers by watching the other interview segments.

The day before the show, call the producer to confirm the time and find out which door you should use, especially if you are on the morning show. (TV station security is quite tight these days.) Also ask if the producer needs any more information.

The Day of the Show

Arrive early, but not early enough to make everyone nuts. Thirty minutes before the show airs should be sufficient (or whatever other time they've given you).

Wear comfortable clothes that don't show sweat. Remember that it's quite warm under those hot lights. Avoid wearing bright white because it can distort color levels on some cameras.

Wear makeup, and make sure to use powder on your face. This goes for men too! If you don't, the bright lights will make you shine and glisten like Nixon explaining those missing eighteen minutes.

Check the back and sides of your hair. The cameras will be taking side shots, and if your hair looks weird, the viewers will concentrate on that and not hear a word you are saying about your book!

While in the bathroom, take deep breaths and hum to warm up your throat. Radio and TV people do this all the time.

Ask to sit in the studio during the show while waiting for your turn. This will help you become acclimated.

Always bring a book for the anchor—they expect it. Also bring an extra copy of your press kit in case the producer misplaced it.

The rest is easy. Go on the air, be yourself, and have a good time. Don't be intimidated by the anchors, and be sure to mention where your next book signing will be. If all goes well you will be ready for prime time!

Getting on Local Prime Time

If you can get on the 6:00 P.M. local news, you have made quite a coup. Your chances for getting a story on the air are about 50/50 if you are from the area or have an exciting local hook. Again, these odds depend on the market. Obviously it is more difficult to get on the air in local news in New York City than it is in College Station, Texas, but any airtime on the 6:00 P.M. news is an excellent use of your time.

The evening news is different from the other news shows in four ways. First, it offers maximum exposure. Second, you will be working with a reporter and a photographer. Third, the interview will be taped before the show so you will not be live. Fourth, its producer has a different mindset. Unlike producers for morning and noon shows, who usually don't care if an author shows up on other stations in the market, an evening news producer wants his show to be the only one in the market to cover the story.

Target Your Station Carefully

You should already know which station has the highest ratings from your previous research, but go ahead and talk to the reporter from the local newspaper who covers the media once more. Confirm which evening news show has the highest ratings or share of the market, which station is most likely to cover your story, and which reporter would be the one to do it.

Make Contact

Send your press kit to the reporter or, as a second choice, the producer. Follow up with a phone call a few days later. At that point, there will be two things the reporter or producer will be looking for: (1) a local angle (or hook); and (2) b-roll (visuals to enhance the interview). First, let's take a look at the hook, the peg upon which the reporter will hang his story.

A logical local hook is that you are from the area. That's a *natural hook*. When you are from out of town, you have to make your own artificial local hooks. To create an *artificial hook,* you can:

- Give a reading at a children's center, nursing home, or hospital.
- Give a talk to high school students about writing as a career.
- Visit an elementary school and help teach kids to write a story.
- Plan a cool event or fundraiser with other local writers.
- Look for ways in which your book is topical (as in our previous President Cleveland's birthday example).

The second thing they're looking for is *b-roll*. What is it? *B-roll* is the word used to describe the pictures you see on the television screen that entertain you while you hear someone's voice talking in the background. These pictures are vital to a story. Linda Ellerbee, famous news anchor and pundit, has said that visuals are absolutely essential for entertaining television. She says: "If the pictures don't contribute anything, well, we have a name for that. We call it radio!" It is in your best interest to make a list of things the photographer can film and have these things ready on the day of the interview. The reporter may already have some ideas, but your suggestions and preparations will be welcome! No reporter wants to do a piece that only shows a talking head. Appropriate b-roll for your story can include:

- The place where you write at your computer (if you're not local, bring your laptop so they can show you writing)
- Any cards, boards, notes, or drawings you made while writing
- The galleys, rough drafts, and outlines
- All of the rejection letters you received (you can tear them up on camera!)
- A favorite scenic place that inspired you to write
- People the reporter can interview, such as fellow writers or bookstore owners
- A local book signing or school speech you've arranged

Remember also that the reporter is writing a story and needs a logical beginning, middle, and end. You should have something visual to represent each element. In Karen's TV interview, some of the b-roll showed her sketching out the plot line of her novel on a large piece of posterboard; meeting with her writers group in a restaurant; and yes, tearing up her rejection notices and throwing them into her fireplace.

At the Interview

If the reporter agrees to do your story, know that his time is limited. Let the reporter choose the most convenient time and place to meet. Bring all your materials—including a copy of the book and an extra copy of the press kit—with you. Help the reporter arrange any other interviews that relate to your story, such as an interview with the bookstore or your writing mentor. Keep in mind that the story will probably last a whopping ninety seconds, so keep your answers brief and to the point. Wear makeup or at least powder. Do not wear a bright white shirt, because it can mess up the camera's color levels. Smile. Twinkle. Look excited about what you have accomplished. Keep eye contact with the reporter, and do not look at the camera, unless you want to appear goofy.

Also remember that, on the evening news, at the end of each story, the anchor usually "tags it out." That's when the actual story ends and the news anchor adds a few words to finish up the piece. These words are always scripted, so make sure the reporter knows the date of your next book signing and where the book can be purchased so that information can be included in the anchor's tag.

After the Interview

Once the interview is over, make sure the reporter knows where to reach you just in case there are some last-minute questions before the story airs. Ask if you can have the b-roll when the editor is finished with it. This is not usually possible, but sometimes they'll agree, and then you can use it for other publicity. Be sure to ask when the story will air. Know that your story may get bumped to another show if there is breaking news. The rule in television news is: "If it bleeds, it leads." So, unless you have a good car crash somewhere in your story, your piece might be pushed to another time or date.

You may want to give the reporter a blank videocassette and ask if you can get a copy of the segment. This can be a big hassle for the reporter, so your best bet is to tape the segment as it airs. Be sure to ask your friends to do the same in case you are like us and can't figure out how to program your VCR. If you are in another city, see if your local friends can tape it, or ask the manager of the bookstore where you did a book signing to tape it for you. If you are staying in a nice hotel, they might arrange to do it for you.

Another option is to contact a local *dubbing service*. This is a business that runs tape on all of the local television news shows and will dub your story onto a VHS tape for a fee. In Norfolk, Virginia, a firm called TV News Clips does this. Ask the television station about the local dubbing service or whether the station itself offers such a service. When you get a copy, be sure to send one to your publisher, who may be able to use it at bookseller conventions or similar promotional gatherings.

Television: National Markets

Every author dreams of the big break—getting on a national television show to promote his book. Stories abound about how a single, two-minute conversation with an unknown author catapulted a book onto the bestseller list. Major talk shows have the power to sell millions of books. You have to realize, however, that every publisher and every author is vying for the same few minutes of national television exposure. So it is critical that you think of every possible avenue, hook, or idea that will make you and/or your book stand out in the crowd. In spite of the overwhelming odds against it, persevere and make sure that your books and press kits are sent to producers at national shows who might be interested in your work. Even one big moment on a national show can sell thousands, perhaps hundreds of thousands, of copies of your book.

Choosing the Show

You may already have several talk shows in mind: ones you think might be interested in interviewing you about your book. Now is the time to think of a national hook, not a local one. What is on the nation's agenda at this point? What is in the news? Is there anything that you could play off of with your book?

Watch the shows you are interested in carefully. Note the topics that seem to interest the host. Some shows deal with timely news topics and others deal with topics of human interest. Have a pencil and paper ready, and pay attention to the credits. (You may wish to videotape these programs so you can review the credits more than once.) There you will find a great deal of information about producers and production companies, especially in the case of syndicated programs. You can also go to a search engine on the Internet and type in the name of the program. The official Web site will be listed, and all the information you need will be right in front of you.

Similarly, the addresses for the major networks are relatively easy to access. Use the following main numbers to find your way to the specific shows you are interested in:

- **ABC:** (212) 456-7777
- **NBC:** (212) 664-4444
- **CBS:** (212) 975-4321
- **PBS:** (703) 739-5000

You can locate the hosts of and producers for the national talk shows by ordering *The Top 250 TV/News/Talk/Magazine Shows*. This book is available from:

Ad-Lib Publications
P.O. Box 1102
Fairfield, IA 52556-1102
Phone: 1-800-669-0773 or 515-472-6617
Fax: 515-472-3186

Use Your Contacts

Use your local television contact to network into the realm of producers and reporters at the national level. Sometimes just having a specific name is a great advantage. At the very least, get the number and name of the show's producer and go through the same steps as you have done for the local television markets. Just remember, you are focusing on a national hook, not a local one.

Once you have been on a local television show, ask the reporter/producer to help you get on their network affiliate morning show. For example, if your story aired on a local ABC affiliate, then *Good Morning America* would be the show to go for. For NBC it would be the *Today Show*, and for CBS it would be *This Morning*. And don't forget about other network and syndicated talk shows, as well as magazine-type format shows such as *The Rosie O'Donnell Show, Dateline, 20/20, Turning Point, The View* with Barbara Walters, and *Oprah* (of course).

In addition to calling the major networks, you can also locate the hosts and producers for national talk shows by going to Belinda Halter's Talk Shows Web site at *www.talkshows.about.com*. This is a fantastic site with a wealth of information.

Local and National Cable TV Markets

While focusing on network television is a must, cable television markets are important too. Cable offers a unique opportunity to target shows that specifically appeal to viewers who might be interested in your book.

Local Cable

Local cable stations will often give you plenty of airtime. Unfortunately, local cable channels don't always have legions of viewers. Nevertheless, your job is to do everything in your power to get the word out, so arrange to do a children's writing workshop and let them tape it. If you do this, be sure to send a note home with each child letting the parents know when the story will air, and ask them to please announce the time and date in their church bulletins or community newspapers. You'd better believe every parent will want every one of their friends to see their children on television. Also ask the local newspaper to come and cover the event. Remember, working all of the angles is necessary.

National Cable

As for national cable stations, Fox has great talk shows and MSNBC and CNN have hours to fill, so try to get on as many of these shows as you can. Figure out an interesting or funny hook. Entice Larry King. Tell Don Imus you want to debate the legitimacy of the romance genre as Karen did. If it's a romance novel, contact the Romance Channel. If you've written a book on fishing, contact TNN or Outdoor Life. If you've written something specifically for women, call Lifetime Television for

Women. The point is that you should look for specific markets that could benefit by what you have to say. The numbers for the major cable networks are:

- **CNN:** (404) 827-1500
- **MSNBC:** (201) 583-5000
- **FOX:** (212) 556-2400

Going after airtime on television, whether local, national, or cable, can be intimidating and can look like an impossible feat. But remember what Woody Allen once said: "Ninety-eight percent of success is just showing up." If your book is not out there and your name is not in front of producers who can help you promote it, then you have a zero chance of getting on their show. Keep at it! You never know when Fortune will smile on you.

Radio: Local Markets

Television is a great way to reach potential readers, but so is radio. Just think about rush hour in Los Angeles. Miles and miles of cars, thousands upon thousands of drivers—a captive audience who, tired of cell phone yammering, are waiting to be entertained by you talking about your book!

Choosing the Station

If you want to be live, on the air, in a radio studio, your best bet is to start right at home, targeting your local market. Call the local newspaper reporter who covers the media and ask which stations have the highest rated shows. You want to find the greatest number of listeners who might possibly buy your book. Again, the ratings will be represented as shares.

Choosing the Show

There are basically two types of radio shows: those concentrating on music, and those concentrating on talk. You can easily promote your book on both.

Most local talk-format radio programs are looking for interesting guests. Listen to several of the highest rated talk shows and find the one you feel best suits the topic of your book. It wouldn't be a good idea to try to promote a darling children's book about saving the whales on the *G. Gordon Liddy Show*. For the greatest number of listeners with the talk format, you want to be on the noon show or the afternoon drive show (4:00 to 6:00 P.M.). And don't forget NPR. They are usually delighted to have authors in for interviews, usually have fantastic interviewers, and the odds of getting on the air are in your favor!

Radio shows featuring music are another breed indeed. Listen to the highest rated shows, noting how much time they might have for a quick interview and book giveaway. Also pay close attention to the type of music you hear. If the station plays country music, they probably couldn't give away a book about the mysterious death of rocker Jim Morrison. To reach the greatest number of listeners, you will want to be on the morning drive show (7:00 to 9:00 A.M.). These shows have the most listeners and are usually formatted for guests and general silliness between songs, news, and weather.

Making Contact

Once you have made your decision, make contact. With radio, you should call first, get a positive response, and then send a press kit. This will save both time and money. Basically, you should think of your phone call as an audition. Most producers will make up their minds whether or not they want you on their show based on what you say. Again, call the producer of the show about fifteen minutes after the show has gone off the air. You will have about three minutes to make your pitch, so quickly—and with enthusiasm—explain who you are, what your book is about, why the book is so very cool, and why it will keep listeners glued to the radio station.

Keep in mind the type of show you are pitching to. When Kathleen pitched *Awakening at Midlife* to the noon talk show "HearSay" on local public radio, she emphasized how a discussion of this book would appeal to listeners who tune in to the talk show/information format. When Karen called the rock station WFAX to promote *Kingdom of Hearts*, she started off by saying that she had a great giveaway for the morning show that would be a hoot. Be sure to speak the language of the station. If you come across as too professorial, you might not get the gig on a rock station, and a wild woman most likely won't end up on the air for a serious talk show.

With either format, you must convince the producer that your book will make good radio, so use the list you made for television, and be sure to include local hooks and gimmicks. The book giveaway is a great idea because it makes the radio station look like they are giving stuff to their listeners. Just don't expect to get paid for the books; radio stations work on very slim budgets.

When the Interview Is Confirmed

Once the interview is confirmed, send your press kit. The producer may ask for your book before making a decision. Go ahead and send it with the understanding that the producer might just want a free book. Once things are set, remember to listen to the show as many times as you can. You want to get used to hearing the host's voice and become familiar with the host's interviewing style. Make a list of things about your book that will

136 ██ Up the Bestseller Lists!

spark interesting conversation or elicit questions, and be sure to take it with you.

The day before you go on the air, call the producer and ask if she needs any more information or whether she has any questions. The reason for this is twofold. First, it makes you appear confident, in charge, and polite. Second, it reminds the producer that you are scheduled to appear the next day. Trust us when we say they might easily forget.

The Day of the Show

On the day of the interview, arrive early. Ask if you can look through the studio window and watch the host at work. This will help to familiarize you with the environment so you will be more comfortable when you are in the studio. Of course for radio, you don't have to put powder on your face, but you do have to sound good, so take a minute before your interview to relax and take deep breaths. Hum to loosen up the vocal cords.

While you are being interviewed, listen carefully to the questions. Radio folks work in a timeframe of seconds, not hours, so make sure your answers are clear and to the point. Be sure to keep eye contact with the host when you are talking, because the best hosts will give you nonverbal cues like smiling and nodding their heads to keep you talking. If a host takes a deep breath as if ready to speak, finish your statement quickly.

Remember, plug your book signing and, if it is your style, make the host appear witty. Also be sure to bring a book for the host, because the producer will probably have snapped up the one you sent!

Giving Interviews by Phone

There is one distinct advantage to radio promotion that television promotion doesn't have, and that is your ability to conduct radio interviews by telephone. With today's digital technology, there is very good broadcast quality when you are interviewed by phone. Additionally, many radio shows are broadcast nationally or regionally into local markets via satellite technology. Therefore, it is quite possible to do several radio interviews that are heard locally in many different cities on the same day, or even at the same time. For example, during the initial publicity for *Awakening at Midlife,* Kathleen was a guest on more than sixty radio shows—ranging from ten-minute interviews to hour-long ones. She never left the privacy of her own home, and at least a dozen of these radio interviews were transmitted to multiple cities via satellite.

How did she make this happen? Publicists at large publishing houses will contact radio stations to pitch you and your book. In the absence of this support, you have the option of hiring an outside company to set up radio interviews for you. There exist a number of companies that work with authors and publishers to set up radio interviews by telephone. On behalf of these authors, the companies send out regular newsletters to radio stations that specialize in talk shows and book interviews. In Kathleen's case, her publisher had an arrangement with one such company, Newman Communications. She was very pleased with their professionalism and productivity. Here's how you can contact them:

Newman Communications
214 Lincoln Street, Suite 402
Boston, MA 02134
Phone: (617) 254-4500
Fax: (617) 254-9583
Web site: *www.newmancom.com*

Check the *Literary Market Place* for other radio producers. Here are two more that are good:

You're On the Air
626-C Admiral Drive, #232
Annapolis, MD 21401
Phone: (800) 594-7748
Web site: *www.pr4u.com*

On The Scene Productions
5900 Wilshire Blvd., Suite 1400
Los Angeles, CA 90036
Phone: (323) 930-1030
Web site: *www.onthescene.com*

Karen worked with On The Scene while she was in TV news, interviewing Warren Beatty, Richard Chamberlain, and Jon Voight. It's a great group.

If you are marketing your book without the advantage of a publicist or major publisher's resources and are watching your budget, you can still target radio shows across the country. Prepare a flyer or brochure describing your book, along with a cover letter indicating your enthusiasm to be interviewed on their talk show. Send it to as many radio stations as you can. To find out which stations might be interested, go to the Web site that offers a guide to over 700 sites: *www.radio.about.com*.

You can also check at the library. The *Literary Market Place* lists 142 radio programs that deal with books and authors. The Internet also has a good directory of radio stations worldwide. Try *http://dir.yahoo.com/News_and_Media/Radio/By_Region*.

Things You Need to Know

Once you have snared your interviews, you are ready to make radio history. But before you go on the air, there are some more things you should know.

First, make sure you understand whether you are to call the studio or they are to call you. Even if they are planning to make the call, be sure that you have their studio number just in case.

Be aware that they will call with very little notice. If you are set up for a 10:00 A.M. interview, they will call about three minutes before the hour, and suddenly, you're on the air.

Listen carefully during the interview. In a studio you can benefit from face-to-face communication, phone interviews provide few clues about the direction in which your host is heading.

If your interview will be broadcast in one particular area only, find something positive to say about the area: "I just love Vermont in the winter," or "I love Jackson; in fact I went to school there for a time." Just make sure you know what you are talking about! If you are broadcasting to someplace that holds only horrible memories, you can always say, "Hey, what can ya say about Jersey City?"

If the program is being broadcast via satellite to several different cities, then *do not* mention the name of a city or state even though that's where your interview is being broadcast from. You will sound like a goof if you talk about how great Key West is in February and the shivering folks in Albany, New York, are listening to you at that same moment.

Use the host's name at least once or twice during the interview, and make sure you know that it is the correct name and how to pronounce it. Call ahead to ask if you have any doubts about either.

As in all media, speak in short concise blocks. We are living in a time of "sound bytes," and it is important to answer questions quickly and to the point if you are going to effectively promote your book via the media.

Answer the questions, but also make sure you convey the information you want your audience to know. With practice it becomes quite easy to reframe a question in order to present the material that is important to you.

Understand that there is a great variability in many hosts' questioning styles. Some are intelligent and thoughtful and will have clearly read your book cover to cover. Others have simply plucked your list of sample questions from the press kit and are slugging through them, one by one.

If you have the option, do not use a cordless or cellular phone. The connection is not as clear. If you must use a cordless phone, stay very close to its home base throughout the interview. Don't go roaming around your house picking lint off the carpet, checking the mail, and so forth. First, you will go in and out of good clear contact, and second, you will become distracted.

If your phone service is equipped with "call waiting," disable it. Murphy's Law indicates that you're likely to get a phone call during your interview. You know how pervasive and persistent telemarketers are. You don't want your listeners to hear that annoying beep that indicates there's another call on the line. There are several ways to disable the feature. When the station calls you, you can put that line on hold and ask them to call you back, thus keeping both lines tied up. Make sure that you arrange this with them in advance so they'll have plenty of time to make the calls before the interview is set to begin.

In most areas, you can also disable the feature by dialing *70 before you dial the number you are calling. In this case, you will be the one making the phone call to the station, so be sure to let them know ahead of time and ask when they need you to call. The *70 approach will disable the feature for that phone call only; after you hang up, it's back to normal. Just remember that if you are interviewing with a number of radio shows, your long distance bill will go up if you are the one making the calls. Methods vary, so check with your local phone company to make sure that you know how to disable the feature, and practice doing so before your interview.

Have a glass of water nearby, and a copy of your book. Hold on to any notes you might need to jog your memory regarding important points, such as when you will be having a book signing in the host's city.

Turn off your radio. This is particularly true if, for some reason, you can receive the show that is interviewing you. If you don't, there's a good chance that your radio will feed back through your phone, making screeching sounds. Even if that doesn't happen, you will be distracted by the sound of your own voice and, excited to hear it, you may begin to stammer and inadvertently miss the questions.

Unless you are the proud owner of a Basenji—an African barkless dog—put all other potentially barking, purring, speaking, rooting, growling, coughing, or whinnying creatures that share your home in another room. This advice comes from personal experience. We've learned that dogs *will* bark at garbage collectors, and they are often not quick enough to figure out why you are giving them savage dirty looks and waving your arms wildly in the air.

The same holds true for humans—little or otherwise. While your friends and children probably won't chew on the phone cord during your interview, they will be excited for you and might distract you with high-fives. Even worse, they may jot down points for you to mention and shove them under your nose.

Radio: National Markets

National radio programs can be as powerful as national television in helping a book to "break out." And once it grabs the public's attention, your book sales can go through the roof. Radio personality Don Imus, for example, personally propelled Jane Mendelsohn's book *I Was Amelia Earhart* toward its bestseller status. Imus's wife, Deirdre, found the book in a discount bin, loved it, and told him about it. For the next two days, he raved about it on his program. The rest is history. So really, you should skip Don and send all books directly to Deirdre . . .

You can make history with your book if you can get a gig on national radio. The NPR news and information show *Fresh Air* concentrates on contemporary arts and issues and often interviews authors. A half-hour interview with host Terry Gross about your wonderful book would certainly increase your sales. A book about television might be the right choice for NPR's Brian Lehrer and his Sunday show *On the Media*. The nationally syndicated Saturday morning show for Public Radio International, *Whad'Ya Know*, has a two-hour talk show/variety/entertainment format that is lots of fun. The witty host, Michael Feldman, often does five-minute telephone interviews with authors and sometimes gives the books away as prizes. This will certainly get your book noticed throughout the reading public.

Be sure to look at the type of book you have. If it is outrageous, you should try to get a slot on the *Howard Stern Show*. If you have written a book about cars or a novel with a misbehaving car as a character, call Tom and Ray Magliozzi (a.k.a. Click and Clack, the Tappet Brothers), and see if they will give you a three-minute phone interview at the beginning of their top-rated NPR Saturday morning show, *Car Talk*. Get on the Internet and check out the National Public Radio site (*www.npr.org*) and the Public Radio International site (*www.pri.org*) for a list of shows.

Getting a booking on national radio, however, is as difficult as appearing on national television. Again, don't give up. You can't win if you don't try. You can't get on any of these shows— radio or television—unless you are willing to spend considerable time and energy in contacting the right people, sending them the right material, and then following up. If at first you don't succeed, try, try again. Your perseverance and a bit of luck is all you need. But if you're not out there trying, then luck doesn't have a chance. Remember the old adage: "The harder I work, the luckier I get."

One last thing to keep in mind with respect to all media, whether it is radio, television, or print, is to try your very best to get copies (videotapes or audiotapes or originals of print material) for your own use. You can include print material in your growing press kit. Videotapes and audiotapes may prove very helpful as you move closer to getting national exposure.

Print Media

People who read books usually like to read about books and their authors. Book reviews and feature articles in newspapers and magazines are a great way to target the 40 percent of our population who buy books.

Local Reviews

Your chances of getting print reviews or feature articles in your local area are far greater than they are of capturing a national review or national feature article. You already have the advantage of being a "local interest," so sit down and make a list of every print medium in your city or area. Every city and town has some kind of local newspaper, but don't forget other local print vehicles. Even the smallest city and town usually has some kind of local magazine, "what's happening around town" periodical, or newsletters directed toward particular markets. Use them!

Local publicity may not sell your book in New York City (unless you're from New York City), but it can do a terrific job of boosting your local book sales and ensuring that your local sign-ings will be successful. Local columnist Larry Bonko of the *Virginian Pilot* newspaper did a wonderful feature article on Karen's *Kingdom of Hearts*. By the end of the following week, the local Barnes & Noble had sold out of her book and had ordered more copies. When the article on *Awakening at Midlife* was printed in the same paper, Kathy had several store managers call to tell her that people were walking in and asking for her book. You may not sell a million copies with local reviews and feature articles, but your sales will certainly increase in the area, and who knows how many of those readers will encourage others to go out and buy your wonderful work.

Call your local Chamber of Commerce and ask if they have a media list available. Be sure to remember the "free" papers— the ones that you can pick up in supermarkets—because they often have a large number of readers.

Read these local newspapers and magazines carefully. Look for two things: (1) the reviewers who write about your type of book; and (2) the reporters who do feature articles on local people making good or who cover the same type of material relevant to your book. Call these reviewers and reporters to introduce yourself and your book. Make sure they know you are a local author. Offer to send them a press kit and a book. Most of them will agree. One week after the mailing, follow up with a polite phone call. Be ready to discuss your list of hooks and angles for the story. Many sites on the Internet also have a good directory of newspapers worldwide. Try *http://dir.yahoo.com/News_and_Media/Newspapers/By_Region*.

National Reviews

National reviews, they say, can make or break a book. And while this is mostly true, it is not always necessarily the case. A while ago, we laughed at the irony in the *New York Times Book Review*, where the editors served up a scathing review of Patricia Cornwell's book, *Hornet's Nest*. They really slammed her. Just above this nasty review was the fiction bestseller list, where her book continued to occupy the number one slot.

James Redfield's *The Celestine Prophecy* has received one horrible review after another in spite of its enormous commercial success. It is generally agreed that the book is not particularly well written and suffers from logical inconsistencies and historical mistakes. The *National Review* called it "a tenth-rate melodrama joining Gnostic hubris with flower-child theology." The *Minneapolis Star Tribune* described it as "New Age pop psychology in the form of a bad novel." Yikes! Do you really want to risk these kinds of blows to your self-esteem? We say, "Why not? No guts, no glory!" Karen remembers that once, during her television news career, a critic reviewed her on-air performance by calling her "cute." After fellow reporters removed the knife from Karen's grasp and hid her car keys, she calmed down and grimly reminded herself of the old adage "As long as they spell your name correctly . . . "

Despite the potential for bad reviews, authors should explore every possible opportunity for publicity. National reviewers include *USA Today,* the *New York Times,* the *LA Times, Time* magazine, and even *People* magazine, to name a few. While there are no hard numbers to support the fact that these reviews increase sales, the exposure to these large audiences should not be underestimated.

Again, don't worry about a negative review. We all know a book or movie critic whose taste is 180 degrees opposite from ours. Remember how Siskel and Ebert used to duke it out weekly over which movies deserved a thumbs-up or a thumbs-down? Any review, even a bad one, is better than no review. Reviews are read by interested readers, and even more important, by book-sellers, distributors, and wholesalers. Good reviews, especially from well known sources, are a powerful addition to your book jacket or cover for subsequent printings. Be sure to photocopy and add them to your press kit as you receive them. You may also fax these reviews directly to book distributors to highlight the attention your book is receiving.

If you are working with a major publisher, the publicity department will usually send out between 300 and 600 review copies of your book. It's estimated that you'll sell 200 orders for every 100 review copies they send out. This normal business expense has publishers budgeting 5 to 10 percent of the first printing for these "giveaways" to national reviewers. Major pub-lishers understand that sending review copies is a matter of course in book sales.

Small publishers, on the other hand, may rely on you to take a great deal of initiative not only in making sure reviewers get copies, but also in helping them develop a list of potential review opportunities.

Finding Review Opportunities

If you are handling most of this responsibility yourself, you will want to make a list of the national magazines and newspa-pers that might be interested. In addition, you should begin to assemble a list of smaller—perhaps lesser known—periodicals that also might be interested in your book. A good resource that can identify review syndicates, book review periodicals, and newspapers with book review sections is the *Literary Market Place* (*www.literarymarketplace.com*). Since the LMP is quite expensive, we suggest spending an afternoon in the library with a photocopier to make lists of potential review sources.

Kathleen worked directly with her publicist in generating a list of potential reviewers that augmented their regular lists. For example, her book was sent to *New Age Journal,* where it received a nice mention in a round-up "Good Reads" column. A press kit and a review copy of the book were also sent to newsletters and journals such as *Common Boundary*, which expresses an interest in the psychology of Carl Jung—the foundational philosophy of *Awakening at Midlife.*

Optimizing Your Timing

Time is critical when dealing with reviewers. They work well in advance. Therefore, unless you have written a book about a breaking news story such as O. J. Simpson or Monica Lewinsky, you want the reviewer to receive a copy of your book BEFORE it is published. Although we emphasize that you should take the long view on marketing your book, reviewers don't take the long view when they review books. They don't like to look at what they consider "old books." Most want to see your book in bound galley form before it is published, and many will only consider a review under those circumstances. In other words, reviewers want the book early, three to four months in advance, the sooner the better.

We cannot stress enough that it is critical to get your book to reviewers as soon as possible. Don't worry that it's in galley form. Bound galleys will note that this is an "uncorrected proof and not for quotation." Reviewers understand that they will be given a final copy of the book from which to draw quotes since the author may make some changes between the bound galley and the final printing. Publicists routinely send a copy of the finished book to reviewers.

Who to Target

Turnover in the publishing field is rampant, so we hesitate to list names, but it is always best to send your package to a *specific person*. No matter who ends up on your list, be sure to send (or to ascertain that your publicist has sent) a cover letter, press release, and bound galleys to the following industry reviewers:

ALA Booklist
American Library Association
50 E. Huron Street
Chicago, IL 60611
Phone: (800) 545-2433
Web site: *www.ala.org*
*Reviews almost any book (7,000 a year) that would be of interest to general public library patrons.

Kirkus Reviews
770 Broadway
New York, NY 10003
Phone: (212) 777-4554
Fax: (212) 979-1352
*Prepublication reviews for booksellers, publishers, libraries.

Library Journal
Managing Editor, Book Review Section
245 West 17th Street
New York, NY 10011
Phone: (212) 463-6819
Fax: (212) 242-6987
Web site: *www.libraryjournal.com*
*Reviews books appropriate for a general public library.

Publishers Weekly
245 West 17th Street
New York, NY 10011
Phone: (212) 463-6758
Fax: (212) 463-6631
Web site: *www.publishersweekly.com*
*The major trade magazine for the publishing industry.

In addition to reviewers for specific special markets (e.g., sci-fi, romance, mystery, children's books), you should send (or make certain that your publicist has sent) review copies and a press kit to the national reviewers listed next. If you do not have a publicist assigned to your book, call these numbers first to ascertain what kind of books they review, and then get the name of the person who reviews your genre (e.g., fiction, nonfiction, children's books, etc.). Call. Get the name of that appropriate person. The following is a list of the kinds of publications that you should be looking at for national reviews. It should be clear that this is not a comprehensive list, only food for thought.

Chicago Tribune Books
435 N. Michigan Avenue, Room 400
Chicago, IL 66011-4022
Phone: (312) 222-3232
*Reviews general fiction and nonfiction.

Los Angeles Times Book Review
Book Review Editor
145 Spring Street
Los Angeles, CA 90053
Phone: (310) 515-5522
*Reviews 2,000 books a year. General fiction and nonfiction.
Note: They do not like follow-up calls.

New York Newsday
2 Park Avenue, 6th floor
New York, NY 10016
Phone: (212) 251-6600
*Daily newspaper, reviews general interest.

New York Review of Books
1755 Broadway, 5th floor
New York, NY 10107-0169
Phone: (212) 757-8070
Fax: (212) 333-5374
*Tabloid for the general public. Reviews 1,000 nonfiction books a year. Also uses excerpts and buys serial rights.

New York Times Book Review
229 West 43rd Street
New York, NY 10036
Phone: (212) 354-3900
*Fiction and nonfiction. Reviews about 3,000 books a year.

San Francisco Chronicle Book Review
Book Review Editor
901 Mission Street
San Francisco, CA 94103
Phone: (415) 777-1111
*One thousand reviews a year. General fiction and non
   fiction. Particularly interested in California authors.

Washington Post Book World
1150 15th Street, N.W.
Washington, DC
Phone: (202)334-6000
Fax: (202) 334-4480
*Up to twenty reviews and features each week.

USA Today
Book Editor
11000 Wilson Boulevard
Arlington, VA 22209
Phone: (703) 284-6000
*General fiction and nonfiction.

Keep in mind that getting reviewed in national magazines or large metropolitan newspapers is quite a daunting proposition. For example, the *New York Times* receives more than *1,000 books per day* for its reviewers. The company employs a full-time person whose only job is to open the packages containing books that come pouring into their mail room and route them to the appropriate reviewer. When you consider that this major newspaper only offers ten to twelve major reviews and only a dozen tiny (one-paragraph) reviews a week—a total of 3,000 reviews a year—you begin to get a sense of the odds against you in getting a national review. Nevertheless, persevere!

The Best Way to Follow Up

Okay, so now you've sent out hundreds of copies of your book and press kits to important reviewers. Ah! Just sit back and wait for the reviews to come tumbling in. Well, maybe not. Again, you have chosen to make your living and your mark in an extremely competitive environment. We suggest that you work with your publicist to make certain that follow-up calls are made. These calls are important and will determine whether your book has been received and whether the reviewer has any intention of reviewing it.

Some publications do not like these kinds of phone calls. However, it is our experience that most reviewers are willing to answer questions about the arrival of your book, though most are frazzled and overwhelmed. So keep your conversation very friendly but to the point. Their offices are filled with books, and a phone call from you or your publicist might just prompt them to take a more personalized look at your book.

If you learn, however, that they do not intend to review your book, nicely ask them to forward it to a feature editor (or an editor in an area that is a good fit for your book). For example, if you've written a book about decorating, the Home and Leisure editor may find your book interesting. If you've written a wonderful novel that involves a Little League baseball team, one of the sports editors may be interested in incorporating something about your book in an article on this topic. Who knows? You might even become identified as an "expert" in the area. Even without a full review, you or your book may be quoted: "Johnny Peso, the main character in Bill Smith's *Little League Daze*, says that the 'fun has gone out of the sport,' and the kids in our neighborhood agree."

The truth is that the reviewer may not send your book along to another editor. Your book may be hidden in an overflowing bin or basket, or it may even have gone straight to the trash. If the reviewer doesn't seem to have your book on hand, simply ask for the *name* of the editor or writer for the appropriate section of the newspaper and send another copy of your book to that person directly.

Internet Reviews

The Internet is another option for book reviews. Finding sites that review books is fairly easy. Get on the Web and surf into the tried and true sites such as Writers Write (*www.writerswrite.com*) and look for the appropriate links. Make sure to choose your Web reviewers with care. Take a look at the site to see if they specialize in a specific genre. Read a few reviews. E-mail them and ask how long they have been around and how many hits they get per month. Contact an author who has recently been reviewed and see what impact the review has made on sales. Some interesting book review sites to get you started are:

Scribe & Quill: *www.scribequill.com*. This site has 200 subscribers and 3,000 hits per month.

BookPage: *www.bookpage.com*. This is a monthly book review distributed nationwide through more than 2,000 bookstores and libraries. All reviews are also posted on their Web site. They like to receive books three months before the publication date and prefer those with national distribution.

BookBrowser: *www.bookbrowser.com*. This site had 850,000 visitors in 1999 and averages 2,700 hits per day.

Columns and Articles

As an author, you should also investigate opportunities to write articles on the same or a similar subject as your book. This will give you another chance to put your name in front of readers. And, as a writer, certainly you will find a creative way to reference your book in the article!

Finding the Right Publication

Send queries to appropriate magazines or newspapers. Kathleen submitted a query to a regional news magazine for an article called "Blooming in Life's Second Half," an upbeat look at the opportunities for growth and change that midlife offers, an excellent spin-off from her *Awakening at Midlife* book. In this article, the main points are illuminated by stories of real people—some well known—who made major life changes during midlife. Want a sample? Did you know that Ian Fleming only began to write the James Bond books when he was in his forties? He was a banker until then. And Julia Child only began to cook, taking her first steps to becoming a culinary icon, when she was in her fifties.

Although this article builds on the material Kathleen wrote for *Awakening at Midlife*, "Blooming in Life's Second Half" is *not* an excerpt from the book. (We will discuss excerpts in the next chapter.) Instead, it is a newly written article designed to appeal to the readers of this particular magazine. However, the article references *Awakening at Midlife*, and the fact that Kathleen is the author of this book will appear in the short description of her that follows the article. In addition, Kathleen also submitted the query for her article to an in-flight magazine with a distribution of 440,000 and a readership of 2.3 million. Plenty of folks interested in the subject of midlife travel by air, and a plane makes for a nice captive audience. Kathleen submitted multiple queries, and you should do the same. When you receive positive responses, pick the best one, then write the article so it conforms to the magazine's specific guidelines.

So while you're at the library researching your next book, look at the kinds of magazines and other publications that might have an interest in your book or at least the material your book touches on. If you wax poetic about food in your book, like Lawrence Sanders did in his "Deadly Sins" novels, *Food and Wine* magazine might be interested in an article about your culinary exploits. If your book is about growing up as an African-American child in an all-white neighborhood, *Ebony* magazine could be interested in an article relating to this experience.

Look through reference books about magazines, too. One of the most popular ones is *The National Directory of Magazines* (212-741-0231). You might also want take a look at *The International Directory of Little Magazines and Small Presses* (*www.dustbooks.com/lilmag.htm*).

Better still, go to a large bookstore, newsstand, or library, and write down the names of appropriate magazines. Don't neglect your own local and regional magazines and newspapers, either. It is often easier to sell your article to small-market publications, and remember, you are your own local hook. Also, be sure to target any publications of organizations with which you are associated: alumni, trade associations, and so forth. The Web site (*www.newspapers.com*) has links to newspapers, trade journals, business publications, specialty publications, and college and university newspapers. And check out the Association of Alternative Newsweeklies at *www.aan.org,* a trade association of over 120 non-daily newspapers.

Obviously, the best of all possible worlds is when you get paid for an article. But if you have explored all those options and none of them have come to fruition, we suggest offering an article to magazines or newspapers for free. So long as the article includes your *tag*, which gives your name and the title of your new book, there is benefit to be had. Also consider writing an op-ed piece or letter to the editor. Find a legitimate link to some stories that are in the public's mind, and write the piece, noting that you have written a book on the topic at hand.

Finding Your Hook

Once you've found the right publication, read the *masthead*, the section at the beginning of the magazine that lists current information on editors' names and the address of editorial offices. Very often, there will be information about submitting articles. Most magazines will send you a copy of their "Writers' Guidelines" if you send a short note requesting those guidelines and a self-addressed, stamped envelope (SASE). Within a few weeks, you'll receive information that describes the kinds of stories they are interested in buying, length of submissions, payment ranges for various kinds of articles, and so forth. Carefully read these guidelines before sending a query to the editor. In short, you are becoming educated about what they are looking for.

Next, go to the library and look through the previous twelve months of issues for that magazine. You don't want to submit a query for an article they already did in the past year. Get a good feel for whether or not this is the kind of publication that would be interested in an article on the topic you are proposing. Editor after editor have complained that they routinely get query letters from writers who have obviously never read their magazines. This is not only insulting to the editors, but a waste of your time and energy because you're pursuing bad leads. In other words, if you have written a cookbook detailing your favorite Southern rib recipes, please don't send a query to *Vegetarian Times!*

This example highlights another recurring point: the issue of hooks. In some ways, it is easier for nonfiction writers to develop interesting spins on their topics, reframing them so they will be of interest to various magazines or newspaper editors. However, fiction writers can always find ways of looking at their characters, settings, plot lines, and so forth that can be translated into a magazine article. For example, if you have written a novel that takes place in Atlanta, you may want to write an article about Atlanta and why this is the only city in which your fiction could have taken place. Travel magazines, in-flight magazines for airlines that service the Atlanta area, regional Georgia magazines, and local publications serving Atlanta might have an interest too.

Let's say your children's book focuses on a pig as the main character. Can you also write a short article about how children relate to animals in stories? Adults, especially book editors, often argue against "anthropomorphizing" animals (giving them human characteristics). Yet, child readers seem to disagree seriously and strongly. Perhaps you could conduct a short survey with neighborhood children, asking them how they relate to animals in stories. Their comments, included in your article, could add depth and interest to this subject.

Look for interesting, creative approaches to extend your book to new markets. Remember, you really want readers of the magazine to know that you have written a book, become familiar with its title, and become interested in reading more of your work. And don't think that just because you are a fiction writer you can't write a nonfiction article! After all, you are a *writer,* and stretching yourself in new ways will only enhance your skills. Two books that might help you get started in writing magazine articles are:

> *The Complete Guide to Magazine Article Writing*, by John M. Wilson. Writers Digest Books, 1993.

> *The Magazine Article: How to Think It, Plan It, Write It*, by Peter P. Jacobi. Indiana University Press, 1997.

Remember that the greatest promotion your book can receive is to have lots of people know about it. Television, radio, and the print media are out there just waiting for your book!

Points to Remember

- Choose the local television or radio station with the best ratings.
- Choose the local television or radio show that fits your book.
- Local cable stations will often give you plenty of airtime.
- Press kits are your best approach to television.
- Phone calls are your best approach to radio.
- For local television, focus on local hooks and visuals.
- For local radio, focus on local hooks and gimmicks.
- Make it easy for the television reporter, and fun for the radio host.
- Watch or listen to television or radio shows before you go on the air.
- You can interview on radio in different cities on the same day.
- Use local television contacts to network to the national television level.

Points to Remember,
continued

- Your chances of getting print reviews or feature articles in your local area are good.
- Any national print review, even a bad one, is often better than no review.
- The national reviewer should receive a copy of your book three to four months before it is published.
- Articles in national magazines and large circulation newspapers provide a powerful way to promote your book.
- Investigate opportunities to write articles on the same or a similar subject as your book.
- Nonfiction writers can develop interesting spins on their topics.
- Fiction writers can translate plot lines, characters, or settings into interesting articles.
- You can offer an article to magazines or newspapers for free as long as the information on you and your book is included in the tag.

8

Selling Rights

In book publishing, the primary right is the right to publish your book. This is the right that you sold when you entered into a publishing agreement. But there are other rights, indeed a "bundle of rights," that can be sold as well. Collectively, these rights are referred to as *subsidiary rights* or *sub-rights*, in the language of the publishing industry.

Subsidiary Rights

Basically, subsidiary rights give someone else your permission to repackage or reproduce your book. Some of these subsidiary rights include: first and second serial rights; paperback, including mass market paperback rights; foreign translations; anthology; electronic; audio (both abridged and unabridged); movie and television; book clubs; and merchandising (e.g., Hasbro wants to make 12-inch action figure dolls based on your main character).

Because subsidiary rights are so important and can generate so much income, most major publishers rely on the support of entire departments devoted to the sale of these rights. Let's first take a look at the benefits of some of these rights:

1. The sale of subsidiary rights generates income.
2. The sale of first serial rights (excerpts released *before* the book is published) can create advance interest in your book, which is likely to generate larger orders from bookstores.
3. Second serial rights (for excerpts *after* the book is published) offer your book good publicity after it hits the stands.
4. The sale of television or movie rights creates additional book sales when the movie is released or the television show airs.
5. Your book gains credibility by the sale of rights.

Rights Defined

Now let's take a look at exactly what these rights are. It is easiest to think of subsidiary rights if we divide the rights into two basic categories: print rights and nonprint adaptations.

Print Rights

Print rights include mass market reprint rights, periodical rights (first and second serial rights), condensation rights, anthology rights, book club rights, British rights, and translation rights. Check in the *Literary Market Place* for listings of and additional information about subsidiary rights. Generally, when these print rights are sold, the author splits the revenues or royalties with the publisher. It should be noted, however, that typical publishing agreements often allow the author to retain a variety of subsidiary rights. The sales of any subsidiary rights should be clearly spelled out in the publishing agreement. Your agent should work to sell the rights retained by you, the author. The following is a listing of industry standards for print rights:

Type of Print Rights	Portion to Author	Portion to Publisher
Paperback Rights	50%	50%
Book Club Rights	50%	50%
Foreign Language Rights	75%	25%
British Rights	80%	20%
First Serial Rights	90%	10%
Second Serial Rights	50%	50%

Note: All rights and the splits should be clearly defined in your publishing contract.

Nonprint Adaptation Rights

Nonprint adaptation rights have traditionally included stage, radio, film, television, and audio rights. Today, new rights based on present and future technologies are also being sold, and details on exactly how this is done are being developed by the industry as this book goes to print. For example, rights for books are also being sold as "electronic" rights (e.g., the repackaging of your material for the Internet) or multimedia rights (e.g., electronic books on CD-ROM). Within the new area of electronic and multimedia rights, we can think of two categories: verbatim and adaptation rights. For example, verbatim rights would include the exact reproduction of your book using a new technology—such as when your book is reproduced on the Internet or on a CD-ROM. On the other hand, adaptation rights would use some part of your book as an inspiration for a product or a part of a product, such as if your science fiction novel establishes the groundwork for a CD-ROM game. In the second case, although your characters and setting would be part of the game, the game itself would not include the actual text of your book.

There is still much to be worked out concerning the rights for these new technologies, and revenues or royalties vary. At this point, no industry standards have been agreed upon. Rights based on new and emerging technologies are complex, and all serious authors should keep up with developments in this area by regularly reading *Publishers Weekly* and other trade journals.

Perhaps the greatest area of interest in subsidiary rights for writers—especially fiction writers—exists in the possibility of film or television rights. You may have already envisioned your novel becoming a major motion picture. Perhaps you even wrote the characters by imagining particular actors playing the roles. In Karen's novel, the character of the evil Duke Richard was based on actor Alan Rickman, and not surprisingly, people have made just that comment after reading the book. Hollywood and the television industry, especially since the advent of cable, are hungry for material they can turn into films and television shows. The sale of these rights can be very profitable for authors. Most publishing contracts give 100 percent of nonprint revenues to the author (although in a few cases, the publisher will retain

10 percent as an agency fee and give 90 percent of the revenues to the author). Even if the publisher doesn't receive a percentage of the revenues, they will certainly profit from the publicity a movie deal will create.

You should have a long conversation with your publisher and/or literary agent about the selling of subsidiary rights and about developing strategies to do so. These conversations are best held before you sign either an agent contract or a publishing contract.

Selling Rights

You should never enter into any agreement for any rights, especially film or television rights, without the intimate involvement of your literary agent and/or a literary attorney. Film and television rights may be worth millions of dollars, and it is critical to negotiate a good contract (e.g., you want a percentage of the gross, NOT the usual 15 percent net).

The first step in selling rights usually involves options. An option is a temporary agreement for exclusive rights to your work. The agreement is for a limited amount of time, anywhere from six months to two years, and it keeps your work out of circulation while the producers try to put together a deal. If the option expires with no deal in place, you keep the payment and the rights are returned to you. If a deal is made, you keep the payment, they keep the rights, and you negotiate for the sale of permanent rights.

Fiction Rights

Here is the good news for fiction writers! Film and television rights are far more likely to be sold for works of fiction.

While many films and television movies are produced from original screenplays, novels and short stories also provide the basis for some of these productions. Selling rights for film and television movies offers enormous opportunities for writers. For example, Nicholas Evans wrote *The Horse Whisperer* and sold the movie rights for this book, his first novel, to Robert Redford for an undisclosed sum. (It is generally thought to be around $1.5 million—a nice piece of change!) And once the movie was released, book sales skyrocketed, just as they did for Isak Dinesen's *Out of Africa,* Tom Wolfe's *The Right Stuff*, William Styron's *Sophie's Choice*, and every Jane Austen book ever written.

These examples highlight the synergy between book publishing and film or television adaptations. Once you have had a successful film made from one of your books, Hollywood continues to look at your work with interest. Consider this: The film adaptation of Warren Adler's *The War of the Roses*—starring Kathleen Turner, Michael Douglas, and Danny DeVito—was a box-office smash in 1989. Since then, seven more of his novels have been bought or optioned for films, with two currently under development at Columbia and Warner Brothers. Interestingly, Adler's agent was successful in selling the film rights for his next book—*The War of the Roses: The Children*—even *before* offering it to publishers for publication as a book. Plus, Adler has been hired to write the screenplay. Yowza! Obviously, the selling of rights can get you closer to sipping those frozen drinks while basking under the sun in the islands.

As you can see from this example, the relationship between book publishing and films is very close; original screenplays are often written first, and then publishers buy the rights to adapt the screenplay to novel form. *Rocky*, the first three *Star Wars* films, *Raiders of the Lost Ark*, and *E.T.* were all originally written as screenplays. All have been adapted to book form. In the television venue, original teleplays for the *Star Trek* series, *JAG*, and *Xena: Warrior Princess* have spawned a whole industry of books based on the show's characters.

Nonfiction Rights

Now here is the good news for you nonfiction writers. Although it is unusual for nonfiction books, with the exception of some biographies or truly remarkable stories, to be made into films or television shows, there are some notable exceptions. In fact, more and more films are being made based upon true stories that were originally penned as nonfiction books. Just take a look at movies released in the past several years, such as *The Perfect Storm, A Civil Action,* and *Angela's Ashes*. Kathleen sold television rights to Public Broadcasting for an hour-long special based on her nonfiction book *Awakening at Midlife*. Michael D'Orso's book *Like Judgment Day: The Ruin and Redemption of a Town Called Rosewood* detailed the destruction of a black community located along Florida's Gulf Coast during the 1920s. This book became the basis for a screenplay and a successful movie starring Jon Voight called *Rosewood*. Similarly, a television movie was made depicting author and explorer Jon Krakauer's riveting firsthand account of a catastrophic expedition climbing Mount Everest. Both the television movie and the book were titled *Into Thin Air* and proved very successful.

Serial Rights

Articles in national magazines and major newspapers provide a powerful way to promote your book. Publishers understand this and attempt to sell first and second serial rights for their books to these publications. First serial rights give a periodical the exclusive right to publish either excerpts from or a serialization of your book *before* it is published. Because the magazine gets to print your work first, these rights are purchased for larger sums of money than second serial rights, though the payment may range anywhere from $400 to $200,000 or more. The days of staggering prices for first serial rights seem to have waned, but some deals were doozies in the past. For example, *Woman's Day* paid $200,000 for the exclusive rights to excerpt *Times to Remember*, Rose Kennedy's autobiography. First serial rights for Lee Iacocca's autobiography were purchased by *Newsweek,* and the resultant prepublication publicity launched this book into one of the first mass market hardcover bestsellers. However, unless you are a well known author or have some startling news to reveal, selling first serial rights can prove quite difficult for new authors.

Second serial rights (or *reprint* rights) can be sold before a book is published but cannot be printed until after the book has been released. Obviously, these rights are not as valuable as the first serial rights because the magazine purchasing them will not have "scooped" anybody. Furthermore, these rights are generally *not* exclusive rights and can be sold and resold to other publications.

Prices for the sale of second serial rights range from $50 to $2,000. For these rights, the most important thing is not the money but the promotion gained for your book. Publishing excerpts from your book can be a powerful way to get it in front of potential readers. People who read your excerpt and like it will go out and buy the book. For example, Kathleen's publisher sold second serial rights for a chapter from her *Awakening at Midlife* book to *Natural Health* magazine, and many of its readers were encouraged to want to buy the book to read the rest of it!

If your publisher has not succeeded in selling the second serial rights to your book, you might want to discuss the idea of giving these rights away. What?? Why would you want to give anything away? Again, excerpting or serializing your book will help you reach new markets of readers who will then go out and buy your book.

Contract Negotiations

Subsidiary rights are important to authors because they generate income and are very effective in promoting books. It is in your best interest to understand these rights and make certain that you and your agent retain as many of these rights as possible when negotiating your publishing contract. And if you decide to sell them as part of your publishing contract, you will want to know, for a fact, that your publisher has successfully sold these various subsidiary rights for other books before you agree to part with them.

It is important that you not ignore these rights. There are many excellent books about the publishing industry with specific information relating to literary law and subsidiary rights. Several we recommend are:

> *The Copyright Book: A Practical Guide*, by William S. Strong. MIT Press, 1981.

> *Every Writer's Guide to Copyright and Publishing Law*, by Ellen M. Kozak. Henry Holt, 1990.

> *The Law (In Plain English) for Writers*, by Leonard D. DuBoff. John Wiley & Sons, 1992.

> *This Business of Writing*, by Gregg Levoy. Writer's Digest Books, 1980.

> *The Book Publishing Industry*, by Albert N. Greco. Allyn & Bacon, 1996.

Points to Remember

- The primary right is the right to publish your book.
- First serial rights are pre-publication rights.
- Second serial rights are post-publication (reprint) rights.
- Subsidiary rights give someone else permission to repackage or reproduce your book.
- Subsidiary rights generate income and promote books.
- Discuss these rights with your literary agent before signing a publishing contract.

Epilogue: Taking the Long View

Hollywood releases motion pictures with an eye toward the immediate future: a film is released with a great deal of fanfare, and it either becomes a big hit or it's destined for video rentals and foreign release within a few months. The publishing industry seems to adhere to the same philosophy. A book is published. There is an immediate attempt to garner major reviews and national publicity, and it either hits or it doesn't. Within a few months, the publisher has moved on to bigger and better things, and the publicist who just recently bought you that expensive lunch at a posh New York restaurant now takes a week to return your phone calls. No one is trying to be mean to you—it's just that publishers keep their attention focused on the *frontlist*—books that have just been published or are about to be published. Your book is on its way to the *backlist*—books that are previously published, still in print, and available from the publisher.

Wow, you think, I've spent all this time and energy writing my book, and within a month or two the publisher has given up on it. Well, not given up exactly, but not giving it the attention you think it deserves. Most publishing experts urge authors to avoid this Hollywood view of book marketing and, instead, take the same approaches as do marketers of soap and cereal . . . the long view. Don't despair. It is quite important for you to take the long view, and it is here that you, as an eager and enthusiastic author—coupled with a little bit of luck—can make the difference between your book having average (or below average) sales or becoming a profitable seller.

Consider the following.

Barry Sears's book about diet and healthy eating, *The Zone*, was a below-average seller until it was picked up by both Madonna's personal trainer and the coaches for the U.S. Swim Team. These people became very enthusiastic about Sears's new ideas in food metabolism, and they began to spread the word. The book was on the bestseller list since then and has sold millions of copies.

John Gray's *Men Are from Mars, Women Are from Venus* took almost a year from the date of publication to hit it big, and when it did, it spawned a whole industry of lectures, other books, newsletters, and franchises, including a television series and a Las Vegas show.

Toni Morrison's wonderful book *Song of Solomon* sold more copies after Oprah selected it for her Book Club than it did the year it was released (1978).

Papier-Mache Press, a small publisher, sold more copies of *When I Am an Old Woman, I Shall Wear Purple* in 1991 than it did in 1987, the year it was published. It took more than four years to find its audience—mostly by word of mouth.

Lord of the Flies by William Golding sells over 300,000 copies a year because it is used in so many high school English classes.

Kahlil Gibran published *The Prophet* in 1923 and has sold almost nine million copies since then. In 1992, it was on the bestseller list for almost a year.

Marlo Morgan's *Mutant Message Down Under* was self-published, and the author sold thousands of copies herself before the rights were bought by HarperCollins.

Neale Donald Walsch's *Conversations with God, Part One* was published by a very small publishing house in our neck of the woods (Hampton Roads Publishing in Charlottesville, Virginia) and sold more than 100,000 copies by word of mouth before Putnam raced to central Virginia and bestowed a seven-figure advance on the author. Both of these books became bestsellers after a long struggle to be noticed.

Richard Bolles self-published *What Color Is Your Parachute?* in 1972, and in the last twenty-eight years it has sold more than five million copies.

Richard Evans wrote *The Christmas Box* as a gift for his daughters and made twenty copies, which he had bound at a photocopy shop. Within three weeks those copies had been read by 160 people, who began spreading the word about his wonderful story. Encouraged by his family and friends, he submitted *The Christmas Box* to a few publishers, and his book was soundly rejected by each as being "too short and too seasonal." With no other alternatives, he self-published his book and sold more than 250,000 copies by selling it bookstore by bookstore, and by word of mouth. With the amount of that response—achieved without the backing of a big publishing house—major publishers became interested. Simon & Schuster plunked down a $4.2 million advance for the hardcover and audio rights, and since their acquisition, the book has sold millions.

James Redfield's *The Celestine Prophecy* has sold more than 5.5 million copies. In the beginning, Redfield and his girlfriend hand sold 150,000 copies of this self-published book from the trunk of his Honda Accord before major publishers became aware of its growing popularity. After a bidding war, Warner Books signed a contract for the hardcover rights and reportedly paid him an $800,000 advance. After that, Redfield's book stayed on the bestseller list for several years and spawned sequels and a whole range of merchandise (e.g., calendars, journals, newsletters, personalized audiotapes, etc.). Redfield also received multiple offers for the movie rights. He is now working on a screenplay based on his book.

These examples illustrate the importance of perseverance and maintaining belief in yourself. Often the difference between a bestseller and a book that goes nowhere is a little luck and the little extra time it takes for your audience to find you. If you're not out there working, then luck can't find you. Get involved in the promotion of your book. You have worked hard to write it. Now exploit every opportunity you have or can make for yourself.

We believe strongly in making a little bit of effort go a long way. Write back to every reader who sends you a note expressing their love for your book. Let bookstore managers know you appreciate that they stock and sell your book. Send thank-you notes to every producer who put you on a show and every bookstore that sponsored a signing. Do every little thing you can, because it's the little things that pave the way for the big things. We make a habit of doing at least *five things every day* to promote our books, and you can, too. Send out a press release or a review copy, write to a fan, call a producer, or set up an Internet chat.

Give a business card or a bookmark to someone you meet in a taxi. Write a short article and submit it to a magazine. Start right now and keep trying!

Goethe said it better than we ever could:

> *Whatever you can do*
> *or dream, you can begin it.*
> *Boldness has genius,*
> *power, and magic in it.*
> *Begin it now.*

Good advice. Begin it now and Godspeed. See you in the islands!

Appendix A:
Karen Jones

Commonwealth Publications Inc.

"North America's fastest growing mass market publisher"

FOR IMMEDIATE RELEASE
Kingdom of Hearts
Karen Jones
Commonwealth Publications, ISBN 1-55197-223-9

A TWIST OF FATE - AN INNOCENCE TRAPPED

A vulnerable young woman unwillingly thrust into a struggle for power is caught between an evil destructive duke and a handsome but withdrawn king. Beautiful Catherine fights for survival in the exciting new novel **KINGDOM OF HEARTS**.

Brooding King Stefan keeps to his rooms, held captive by tortured memories. At the other end of the palace Richard, Duke of Egravia, spins a web of betrayal and deceit planning to steal the throne. Having gained control over the weak young prince, the Duke continues his devious scheme by trying to seduce Marie, the Prince's wife.

When Catherine bursts on the scene the Duke's plot begins to unravel. Horrified, Richard watches as the King, awakened to life by Catherine's presence, begins to take back his power. While the court is at the hunting lodge, a frantic Richard lures Marie into his plot to kill the King and charge Catherine with the crime. With the King alive but severely injured and Catherine locked in the dungeon awaiting death, the Prince draws upon his inner strength and the wisdom of an ancient duke to save the throne.

Combining her experience as a feature reporter for television news and as an English teacher, *Karen Jones* writes her way into the imaginations and hearts of her readers.

KINGDOM OF HEARTS is a January release from Commonwealth Publications and is available through Commonwealth at 1-800-491-7737 or from your favourite bookstore.

- 30 -

Contact:
Sheldon Staszko, Publicist
Commonwealth Publications Inc., (403) 432-1100 ext. 254

9764 - 45th Avenue, Edmonton, Alberta, CANADA T6E 5C5
Telephone: (403) 432-1100 • Fax: (403) 432-9409 • Toll Free Order Desk: 1-800-491-7737 • E-Mail: lions@worldgate.com
Visit us on the INTERNET at http://www.commonwealthpub.com

Press Release

Karen Jones

Karen Jones is the author of the successful romance novel, <u>Kingdom of Hearts</u> (Commonwealth Publications, 1996), which is the publisher's best selling title for this year.

Author, educator and broadcast journalist, Karen Jones holds degrees in English and education from the University of Virginia. She also holds a degree in state and federal securities law from the Institute of Paralegal Training, Philadelphia, PA.

Karen has nine years of experience in television news at WVEC, an ABC affiliate as an on-air anchor and feature reporter. In addition, working as a series producer she wrote and produced the long-form series "The Haunting of Virginia" which won an Associated Press Award. She also collaborated with the BBC on its award winning series "Pocahontas". Karen's media experience includes stints as an on-air personality at WNOR, WAFX, and WNIS, in both the talk-radio and rock-n-roll radio format. In addition, she has five years experience in the legal department of United Jersey Banks, Princeton. She has also worked for ten years as an education, teaching and writing curriculum in the public schools.

She is presently at work on her second book, <u>The Marcell Glide</u>, a collection of Southern short stories and another romance novel, <u>The Highland Witch</u>, a historical romance novel set in 15th century Scotland is waiting in the wings.

Author Bio

Author Questions

Kingdom of Hearts

Karen Jones

Setting: Fictional country of Gladeshorn, 1500's

Main Characters:

King Stefan of Gladeshorn – powerful, brooding, withdrawn

Catherine – beautiful young woman forced to work in the palace kitchens

Richard, Duke of Egravia – wicked, plotting, scheming, quite a nasty piece of work

Princess Marie – self-indulgent, petulant wife of the prince, enamored of Richard

Prince Edward – young man, unsure of himself, madly in love with his wife

What is the story about?

Which is your favorite character, Stefan or Catherine?

Why did you choose a fictional setting?

You've said you fall in love with your characters. What about the evil Duke Richard? Isn't he too creepy to love?

Can you tell us who was the inspiration for Marie? She's a character almost anyone would love to hate.

How did you write the sex scenes?

Has your mother read Kingdom? If so, what does she think about the sex scenes?

What's the dumbest question anyone has asked you so far?

How long did it take you to write the book?

Did you base any of the characters on people you know?

Did you have to stick to a certain writing schedule?

What famous actor would you choose to play the lead character?

Why did you give this book this particular title?

Author Questions

•• FEATURE RELEASE ••

KAREN JONES

KINGDOM OF HEARTS
KAREN JONES

Kingdom Of Hearts
KAREN JONES

Twist of Fate

Abandoned and alone, beautiful Catherine struggles to survive in the harsh and unfamiliar palace kitchens.

Upstairs, powerful but solitary King Stefan sits brooding about his weak son and the betrayal by his long-dead queen.

At the other end of the palace, Richard, Duke of Egravia, broods about betrayal of another sort. Like an elegant spider, he spins a web of seduction and deceit in his attempt to seize the crown.

A strange twist of fate thrusts Catherine between these two men, her presence fanning the flames of desire and igniting a battle to the death for the throne.

In an ancient kingdom, two men battle for the love of a beautiful woman.

MARKETING:
- SUPER TITLE in Commonwealth's monthly catalog.
- Feature title on INTERNET catalog.
- Mailing to national and regional magazine and newspaper reviewers.
- Book signing tour.
- Promotional posters available.
- North American promotional campaign.
- Special advertising campaign throughout Romance circuits.
- 24-copy floor display with special riser 1-55197-793-1 @ $119.76/167.76 Can. 10" w x 61" h x 13 1/2" d.

TITLE:	**KINGDOM OF HEARTS**		
AUTHOR:	**Karen Jones**	RIGHTS:	**World**
PRICE:	**$4.99/6.99 Can.**	AUTHOR HOME:	**Virginia, U.S.A.**
ISBN:	**1-55197-223-9**	LOCALE:	**Gladeshorn (fictional)**
PAGES:	**378**	BACKGROUND:	**Original**
SPINE:	**12/16**		
CATEGORY:	**Romance**		

Commonwealth Publications Inc. Catalog

Steamy scenes are in forecast

WVEC-TV weather reporter Karen Jones pens a romance novel

Jones does her best writing when the weather is nasty. "I'm fed by cold, gray, rainy, windy days," she says.

KAREN JONES

By LARRY BONKO
TELEVISION COLUMNIST

WELCOME TO the fifth career of Karen Jones, former teacher, former banker, former radio personality, current WVEC weekend weather reporter, and now . . . novelist. Romance novelist.

"Kingdom of Hearts," Jones' first work of fiction, has been published by Commonwealth Publications Inc. of Edmonton, Alberta, Canada. The 368-page softcover novel is in a book store near you.

Look for it in the alone-and-abandoned-maiden-in-a-dungeon, evil-duke, brooding-king, web-of-betrayal-and-deceit, ripped-bodice section.

It sizzles.

"The duke moved his hand further up the inside of her leg, pausing at the top of her thigh, rubbing the soft flesh lightly, teasingly."

Yes, the bubbly woman in short hair you see on WVEC discussing highs and lows on the weekends wrote that.

Karen Jones, you are so wicked.

Jones began the novel about the beautiful scullery maid, Catherine, and the 17th century royalty infatuated with her, about three years ago. She wrote on her days off, doing her best work when the weather was nasty.

"I'm fed by cold, gray, rainy, windy days."

Please see **TV,** *Page E6*

The Virginian Pilot, December 15, 1996

SUNDAY BREAK

TV: Forecast calls for romance

Continued from Page E1

Silence feeds me. Quiet feeds me. The dark of night feeds me," said Jones, speaking not unlike the women in her novel set in a kingdom where, among the noblemen, seducing chaste maidens is a sport second only to hunting wild boar.

She will soon begin another novel. Begin again, I should say.

With "Kingdom of Hearts" on its way to a publisher earlier this year, Jones began a novel about a witch who lived in Scotland ages ago. After writing about 80,000 words, Jones put the novel aside.

"I decided I wasn't in love with the character," she said. But she is all wrapped up in Serah, whose life will be the centerpiece of the second novel, which she will write all over again.

"I'm almost ready to launch," said Jones.

"The slingshot is poised and ready."

On the next cold, gray, rainy, windy day, stay out her way, Hampton Roads. Jones is just about to hit the word processor again — a woman possessed.

"When I start, I can't stop. I don't eat. I don't sleep. I write. Writing takes up most of my life except for work and my relationship with a very understanding man."

And how does she write?

Vividly.

It's not just a shudder in "Kingdom of Hearts," it's an "inward shudder." It's not just a laugh. It's a "kingdom of giggles." Eyes don't just see. They "snap with sarcasm" or "flash hotly."

Jones' characters shudder and shiver throughout.

She's a pretty good storyteller, a gift with which the Jones family is blessed, she said.

"I come from a race of storytellers. I recall lazy summer nights at my parents' tobacco farm in North Carolina when the adults gathered on the front porch to trade stories. My father was such a good storyteller that everyone at the dinner table would fall silent as he spoke."

Even good storytellers need a push now and then, and in Jones' case, it came from writing coach Tom Bird. "He cracked the whip. He said I should shut up and write. After I began, the character of Catherine suddenly showed up. I liked her. I liked writing about her."

Jones grew up in Virginia Beach (Princess Anne High Class of 1969), moved on to the University of Virginia, and then spent six years teaching English. Jones gave that up for the business world — assistant corporate secretary in mergers and acquisitions with a New Jersey bank — before coming back home six years ago.

About that time, she did a radio commercial for a Chinese restaurant that got her noticed by the folks at WNOR-FM. They gave her a job there (why they changed her name from Karen Jones to Karen Smith, I'll never know), and later Jones worked for another station in this market.

That's when WVEC co-anchor Barbara Ciara ran into her. "She thought I sounded good on the radio and looked presentable in person.

Eyes don't just see. They "snap with sarcasm" or "flash hotly."

Barbara said they were looking for a weekend weather chick at Channel 13, and suggested I apply. I said, 'Why not?' "

The news director gave Jones two weeks to prove herself. The teacher turned banker turned radio disc jockey caught on with Channel 13. Great. But she would gladly give up TV to write full-time her novels about ancient castles and dark dungeons and heroines in lace petticoats.

"In a heartbeat," said Jones. "I love my job at WVEC. It's a really cool job, and I have a wonderful time working with wonderful people. But if I could live out in the country, sit silently in a room by myself, and write novels for a living, I'd do it in a minute."

The appetite for romance novels is large, according to figures supplied to the Associated Press by Harlequin Enterprises Ltd. More than 50 million women in North America — average age 42 — read romance fiction. It's a $1 billion industry.

Writing the romance novel was the easy part for Jones. Getting it published was hard. And finding an agent who believes in you is a supreme challenge.

Jones contacted 200 of them before she found an agent who was excited about "Kingdom of Hearts." Many unpublished writers have said this before Jones: "I dealt with a lot of rejection."

Today, Jones has her agent and publisher. She waits for the characters in her new novel to slip into her consciousness with skirts swirling, so she can begin writing about them.

"I close my eyes and I see them play out their lives in front of me. I see who they are, what they are wearing, how they smell. I never know what they will do. They surprise me."

And Jones never knows when the inspiration will come.

The heroine of her second novel popped into her head when she was chopping vegetables for a salad.

Any day now, the words of Jones' new novel will begin to flow from the imagination of this woman who looks very much like Meryl Streep. On the day of the interview, she was in white — snow-white turtleneck, white pants tucked into black boots.

She looked smashing.

Jones is divorced, the mother of a son in college. She is dating a retired Navy captain.

And she is living the life of a celebrity in a TV market where viewers think of Jones and her colleagues as friends and neighbors. "I work in television where I grew up, so I am constantly meeting people I know from high school, from church, from when I taught school.

"I love when they come up to me and speak. But being recognized in public can be uncomfortable at times. I've been in a drug store, picking up pills and have seen people step forward and lean in to hear what the druggist is saying to me.

"One time, I was buying wine in a grocery store when a lady said, 'I'll just have to tell everybody that Karen Jones drinks.' I don't mind that. But what I do mind is being grabbed and kissed."

Strange men grab and kiss her?

"No," said Jones. "It's the women."

If she thought the women out there in TV land were passionate about her before, wait until "Kingdom of Hearts" is out for a while. Jones at her book signings will be swamped with questions from women — and men, too, I'll wager — about fanning the flames of desire.

I borrowed that "fanning the flames of desire" line from Jones' novel. They do a lot of that in the fictional kingdom of Gladeshorn.

THE VIRGINIAN PILOT 12/15/96

The Virginian Pilot, December 15, 1996, continued

Barnes & Noble Announcement of Discussion and Signing

Appendix B:
Kathleen Brehony

Contact: Vicki Flick
          Associate Director of Publicity
          212-951-8421

AWAKENING AT MIDLIFE

Realizing Your Potential for Growth and Change
by Kathleen Brehony, Ph.D.

*"Brehony...defines, explains, and connects Jungian concepts into an understandable
but not reductive framework. . . . A relatively challenging exploration of the
aspects of change at midlife, including spiritual and physical growth."*
-- Kirkus Reviews

There have been scores of books written about the experiences of midlife, but most have
tended to focus on it as a time of out-and-out crisis -- a period of great upheaval that is
only experienced by a portion of people. Others have suggested that it is simply a time
for great opportunity, and ignored the very real suffering that can accompany the midlife
period. In **AWAKENING AT MIDLIFE** (Riverhead Books; September 1996; $24.95
U.S./$32.50 Canada), psychologist Kathleen Brehony offers a fresh perspective on the
midlife journey. She casts a new light on the transition as one marked by physical and
psychological changes that can be emotionally disturbing, but that also offers individuals
the chance to grow spiritually and positively transform the painful aspects of the midlife
experience.

- more-

A DIVISION OF THE PUTNAM BERKLEY GROUP, INC.

Press Release from Riverhead Books

Brehony, a clinical psychologist and psychotherapist, says that the psychological and physical changes that occur at midlife are an unavoidable reality; they're components of a developmental stage that can no more be ignored than can the separation anxiety of a two-year-old, and that is experienced by everyone in some form.

In **AWAKENING AT MIDLIFE**, Brehony shows readers how to successfully navigate the inevitable midlife stage. Translating Carl Jung's ideas and insights into language familiar to the general reader, and using examples from her own and others' experiences in midlife, she illustrates how this critical and sometimes dangerous stage of human development can be used to lead the way to a richer life. Among the topics Brehony discusses are:

> *how to be aware of the promptings of our inner selves and find the necessary ways of expressing them.

> *the differences in the midlife passages of men and women.

> *creative and practical approaches to getting through this time in ways that enhance the opportunity for growth and change.

As America continues to become increasingly middle-aged, **AWAKENING AT MIDLIFE** offers a welcome and much-needed message of hope to those people approaching their middle years.

Kathleen Brehony currently maintains a private practice in Virginia. She has conducted hundreds of professional workshops, seminars and training programs on the midlife passage and other subjects.

# # #

Press Release from Riverhead Books, *continued*

NEWS·FROM
RIVERHEAD BOOKS

MARILYN DUCKSWORTH VICE PRESIDENT, ASSOCIATE PUBLISHER, EXECUTIVE DIRECTOR OF PUBLICITY
200 MADISON AVENUE • NEW YORK, NEW YORK 10016 • PHONE 212·951·8466 • FAX 212·532·9473

Contact: Vicki Flick
            Associate Director of Publicity
            212-951-8421

ABOUT
KATHLEEN A. BREHONY, Ph.D.

Kathleen Brehony is a licensed clinical psychologist and Jungian-oriented psychotherapist. She holds a Ph.D. and M.S. in clinical psychology from Virginia Tech and a B.A. in Sociology from Catholic University. She completed her residency training at the University of Mississippi Medical Center where she served as Chief Resident. She has taught at the university level and been in private practice for over fifteen years specializing in issues related to transitional developmental periods of life, including midlife and death and dying, as well as the relationship between spirituality and psychology. Throughout her career she has conducted hundreds of professional workshops, seminars, and training programs on these and other subjects. She is especially interested in bringing academic and scholarly information to the general public.

Brehony has published extensively in professional journals and books. She is co-editor of **Marketing Health Behaviors** (Plenum, 1984) and **Boston Marriages** (The University of Massachusetts Press, 1993). She is the author of **AWAKENING AT MIDLIFE** (Riverhead Books, 1996).

Brehony served on the charter editorial board of the journal *Women and Therapy* for seven years and has been guest editor for a number of other professional publications. She has written numerous articles for newspapers and magazines, appeared as a guest on radio and television, and produced and hosted a bi-monthly television interview show, "All About Women." She has co-produced and served as moderator for several television specials for the Public Broadcasting System. Dr. Brehony was the Director of Marketing and, later, President of The Media Works, an independent video and film production company. In addition to her administrative and creative work, she was the head writer for more than one hundred video and film scripts for industry and training.

Dr. Brehony lives in Norfolk, Virginia. She maintains a private clinical practice in Virginia Beach and is working on another book.

# # #

6/96

A DIVISION OF THE PUTNAM BERKLEY GROUP, INC.

Author Bio from Riverhead Books

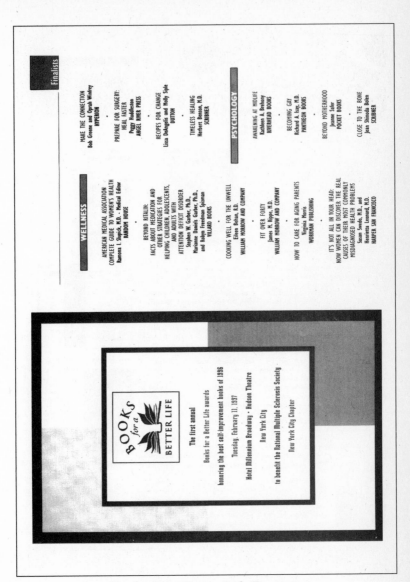

Books for a Better Life Program

G⊙od Reads

More than eighty promising
new books.

By Dan Fields

After looking through scores of publishers' fall and winter catalogues, we've chosen more than eighty titles for your reading pleasure, arranged in alphabetical order:

All of Us: Americans Talk About the Meaning of Death by Patricia Anderson (Delacorte, September). This thought-provoking collection includes interviews with the famous (Isabel Allende, Laurie Anderson, Andrew Weil, M.D.) and not-so-famous.

Anatomy of the Spirit: The Seven Stages of Power and Healing by Caroline Myss (Harmony, October). A medical intuitive and popular lecturer explores the human energy system.

And the Animals Will Teach You: Discovering Ourselves Through Our Relationship with Animals by Margot Lasher (Berkley, December). Let creatures be your teachers, says a psychologist and poet.

At the Heart of It: Ordinary People, Extraordinary Lives by Walt Harrington (University of Missouri Press, September). These sixteen moving profiles originally appeared in the *Washington Post Magazine*.

Awakening at Midlife: Realizing Your Potential for Growth and Change by Kathleen A. Brehony (Riverhead, September). A Jungian-oriented psy-

chotherapist shows how the midlife transition can lead to a richer life.

Betrayal of Science and Reason: How Anti-Environmental Rhetoric Threatens Our Future by Paul R. Ehrlich and Anne H. Ehrlich (Island Press, October). The Ehrlichs (*The Population Explosion*) decry the backlash against environmental policies.

The Call by David Spangler (Riverhead, January). A leading new age thinker considers what motivates, inspires, and sustains us.

Chicken Soup for the Woman's Soul: 101 Stories to Open the Hearts and Rekindle the Spirits of Women by Jack Canfield et al. (Health Communications, October). This cheery compendium includes pieces by Maya Angelou, Bessie Delaney, Robert Fulghum, and many more.

Child of the Dawn: A Magical Journey of Awakening by Gautama Chopra (Amber-Allen, September). The literary debut of Deepak Chopra's college-age son is a tale of India based on his father's *Seven Spiritual Laws of Success*.

Claiming the Spirit Within: A Sourcebook of Women's Poetry, edited by Marilyn Sewell (Beacon, November).

New Age Journal

PROFILE

Crisis Management

She wrote the book on keeping midlife from making you crazy

by Karl Bermann

A psychologist based in Hampton Roads, Brehony had a midlife crisis that spurred her to write a book to help others.

You're in the back seat of a car, driver unknown, careening along a precipitous mountain road. Through cloud-obscured vistas you see the outlines of steeples and oddly shaped buildings. The car becomes transparent and you watch in horror as the tires hit a patch of gravel and the car skids over the edge, into the abyss.

Is it possible? Could you have missed the warning signs that said, "Danger, Midlife Crisis Ahead"?

You wake, breathless and paralyzed.

Midlife crisis. It's scary, but don't panic. Your life isn't half over, it's only half begun, says Norfolk psychologist Kathleen Brehony. Brehony is the author of a new book from Riverhead/Putnam, *Awakening at Midlife: Realizing Your Potential for Growth and Change*, due at bookstores Sept. 10.

Seven years ago Brehony had the dream above, just before she plunged into her own midlife crisis. Dreams like hers are common in midlife she learned subsequently from her clinical practice. But at the time she wasn't prepared, even though she'd been a psychotherapist for years.

There were other warning signs: pressure in her chest and a rapid heart rate. She went to her doctor for an EKG, but the doctor said she was fine.

"I think my body knew that things needed to change," she says. "It had to act out some of that fear and fright that was upcoming."

Then it struck.

"On my 40th birthday I went from knowing exactly who I was and what life was supposed to be to having the rug ripped out from under me." Inside a three-day period Brehony had left a 10-year relationship, fallen in love with someone new, and lost her job.

"I was terrified. I felt like a deer in the headlights of a car. On the surface I looked OK. I wasn't babbling and I wasn't institutionalized, but inside I had no idea who I was or where I was going."

She had always been successful at what she chose to do. A focused, goal-oriented person, suddenly she'd become passive. She felt hopeless and depressed, had bouts of crying. It took her years to regain her sense of equilibrium, she says, to understand what had happened and who the new person was that emerged from the old.

Once her personal crisis was behind her,

however, she could recognize and understand the symptoms in others. In *Awakening At Midlife*, Brehony draws on the experience of her own crisis as well as that of her patients.

Children have stages of development — "terrible twos," adolescence, and so on — but then they grow up and become adults, and that's the end of development, we think. From there we just keep getting older and wiser until we begin to decompose.

Wrong, says Brehony. Midlife is a stage of development too, a stage that's "hard-wired in."

"The thing that makes it different from other developmental stages," she says, "is that somewhere in the back of our consciousness we know

> *"If you've been told, 'Life is tough, there's no time for frivolity,' you may throw out your creativity."*

that life is half over. We hear Peggy Lee singing in the background, 'Is that all there is?'" Midlife is where we realize the fragility of our existence. That's part of what makes it a crisis.

The other part is what Brehony calls "a deep inner energy striving to be expressed."

"We're born whole, but parts of our real selves get shunted off. Aggression and sexuality often get put into that dark area of unconsciousness."

Society requires that some things be suppressed, but often parts of us get buried that are essential for our wholeness. Inside the highly controlled, introverted accountant may be an extroverted, freedom-loving guitar player.

"If you grow up in a family that says, 'This is a dog-eat-dog world,' you may lose your com-

passion along the way," Brehony says. "If you've been told, 'Life is tough, there's no time for frivolity,' you may throw out your creativity. In midlife these parts of the self demand to be known."

Very often, the anxiety, unhappiness, or ennui associated with midlife do impel people to externalize interior changes in inappropriate ways — to make changes simply for their own sake — to leave marriages or jobs whose potential simply hasn't been explored fully. That's where the stereotypes come in, the sports cars, the affairs.

But Brehony says that for many the midlife crisis won't be a crisis at all in the sense we usually think of it. Instead it will come as a vague feeling of emptiness and melancholy, a feeling that life is over.

In her book she provides analysis of midlife in what *Kirkus Reviews* called "an understandable but not reductive framework," along with exercises aimed at easing the way through the crisis and strengthening personal development.

While it's easy to focus on the pain, terror, and trauma that midlife can bring, Brehony says, *Awakening At Midlife* shows that it can also be a "glorious opportunity for change and transformation, for getting in touch with deeper self, for becoming someone with a more deeply felt sense of relationship to others and to life in general." A more soulful person, one might say.

"For me it was a spiritual transformation," she says, "and I see that often in the people I work with. It opened up a whole new sense of how life was to be lived. I think I'm happier now than I've ever been in my life."

She ought to be. The prepublication reviews of her book have been good and she's planning another, about people who perform good works.

She's also learned how to play guitar. ∎

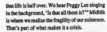

Port Folio Magazine

in wartime D.H. Lawrence country, postwar military service abroad in Malaya and the expatriate literary (and amorous) ambience in France and Spain. Although the narrative closes with the making of the author's reputation, the understated manner of its telling is at odds with the vivacity of his earlier memories. *(Sept.)*

AWAKENING AT MIDLIFE:
Realizing Your Potential for Growth and Change
Kathleen A. Brehony. Riverhead, $23.95 (384p) ISBN 1-57322-024-8
Groundbreaking books like Gail Sheehy's *Passages* have shown that adults, as well as children, navigate major developmental stages. Many people still view the "midlife crisis" askance, however, believing that it consists of red sports cars for men and empty-nest syndrome for women. Jungian psychologist Brehony argues passionately that the midlife transition is a painful period in which ways of coping that served well during young adulthood crumble. She insists that all adults confront the midlife transition, though it is often diagnosed as isolated instances of depression or anxiety. During midlife, she explains, a terrifying sense of losing one's identity or a mind-numbing boredom actually herald the imminent breakthrough of a deeper, more powerful self, the potency of which can seem overwhelming. Brehony assures readers that a successful completion of the midlife transit results in a richer appreciation of life, along with the sense that one is living from the core of one's being. She proceeds to outline tools to cope with the crisis, from building support systems to dreamwork and prayer. Some of her suggestions here are familiar, and the Jungian cast of her text may leave cold those who haven't embraced the Swiss psychiatrist's ideas. Brehony speaks eloquently within this particular framework, however, and other Jungians should find much of note here. *(Sept.)*

LEADING CHANGE
John P. Kotter. Harvard Business School (McGraw-Hill, dist.), $24.95 ISBN 0-87584-747-1
Harvard Business School professor Kotter (*A Force for Change*) breaks from the mold of M.B.A. jargon-filled texts to produce a truly accessible, clear and visionary guide to the business world's buzzword for the late '90s—change. In this excellent business manual, Kotter emphasizes a comprehensive eight-step framework that can be followed by executives at all levels. Kotter advises those who would implement change to foster a sense of urgency within the organization. "A higher rate of urgency does not imply everpresent panic, anxiety, or fear. It means a state in which complacency is virtually absent." Twenty-first century business change must overcome overmanaged and underled cultures. "Because management deals mostly with the status quo and leadership deals mostly with change, in the next century we are going to have to try to become much more skilled at creating leaders." Kotter also identifies pitfalls to be avoided, like "big egos and snakes" or personalities that can undermine a successful change effort. Kotter convincingly argues for the promotion and recognition of teams rather than individuals. He aptly concludes with an emphasis on lifelong learning. "In an ever changing world, you never learn it all, even if you keep growing into your '90s." *Leading Change* is a useful tool for everyone from business students preparing to enter the work force to middle and senior executives faced with the widespread transformation in the corporate world. *60,000 first printing; $100,000 ad/promo; dual main selection of the Newbridge Book Club Executive Program; 20-city radio satellite tour. (Sept.)*

AROUND THE ROOF OF THE WORLD
Edited by Nicholas and Nina Shoumatoff. Univ. of Michigan, $29.95 (250p) ISBN 0-472-10741-0
Tashkent and Samarkand, Genghiz Khan and Tamerlane—the very names associated with Central Asia quicken the pulse and conjure up conquests and migrations, daredevil horsemen and jagged mountain peaks luring climbers to glory and disaster. The Shoumatoffs fill in the traditional yak-and-yurt picture with varied expeditions and travel writings. Excerpts from four classics provide glimpses of 1940s Tibet, midcentury Hunza, 1912 Kashmir and Ladakh and Kyrghyz nomads in 1935. The editors' original contribution is the translation of 16 selections by four Russian writers. The dose of Soviet-era mountaineering history may be too heavy for all save confirmed devotees of the sport, but otherwise, the readings are largely accessible, some even lyrical. Botanist Okmir Agakhanyantz writes with charm and humor about a 600-kilometer walk across Tajikistan and grippingly about a landslide in the Pamir region; artist and ethnographer Alexandre Iacovleff recounts with philosophic subtlety a 1930s trip retracing the route of Marco Polo. Fine illustrations convey the area's natural grandeur and cultural flavor. Annoyingly, the reader has to flip between chapters, preface and bibliography to deduce the source of each piece and whether it is a translation or an excerpt. Worse, the single map is sketchy and unilluminating. But once armchair travelers have found Kazakhstan and the Kun Lun in an atlas, they can enjoy an exotic ride. *(Sept.)*

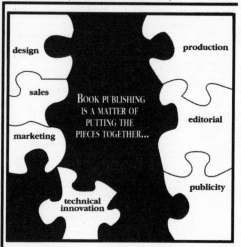

design

sales

marketing

BOOK PUBLISHING IS A MATTER OF PUTTING THE PIECES TOGETHER...

technical innovation

production

editorial

publicity

Publishers Weekly

Another normal stage

*Having experienced her
own midlife crisis,
psychologist Kathleen
Brehony has some advice
for fellow Baby Boomers*

By BETH MACY
STAFF WRITER

Kathleen Brehony was in her early 40s. A relationship she'd been in for 10 years was breaking up. She lost her job — 20 days after closing on a $1,200-a-month home mortgage.

Then she found out her mother was dying of leukemia.

A licensed clinical psychologist, Brehony was more than familiar with the warning signs of the so-called midlife crisis.

"It felt like I was falling off a cliff," the former Roanoker says. "It was not just this internal guilt and anguish, but the sense that life was not going to be what I'd thought it was going to be.

"Most people live as if they'll never have to let go of anything. When the truth is, if you live long enough, you'll have to let go of everything."

That Brehony did let go of everything — and re-emerged much richer for it — is the theme of her story and many others chronicled in her new book, "Awakening at Midlife: Realizing Your Potential for Growth

■ **Kathleen Brehony** will sign copies of her book from 7 to 9 tonight at Books-A-Million at Crossroads Mall and at Ram's Head Books in Towers Mall, 1 to 3 p.m. Saturday.

Awakening at Midlife

*Realizing Your
Potential for
Growth and Change*

Kathleen A. Brehony

PLEASE SEE **BREHONY**/6

The Roanoke Times, November 15, 1999

EXTRA 6　The Roanoke Times, Friday, Nov. 15, 1996

Brehony

FROM PAGE 1

and Change" (Putnam, $24.95).

The book, which hit the shelves in mid-September, is a hit among soul-searching baby boomers, who are turning 30 this year in a sort of 10,000 a day. Brehony believes the book differs from the rest of the self-help fare because it treats midlife as a normal stage of development — not unlike separation anxiety in a 2-year-old.

"A lot of what's out there now [in books] is 'midlife is only rosy, the empty nest, climb-a-mountain sort of thing,' says Brehony, now 47. But that's only half the story.

"The other half is, the universe kicks our a—, and we won't survive these changes simply by acquiring new things. We have to empty our selves in order to pick up anything new . . . I mean, why is it so important to drive a BMW if, in the end, you're gonna die?

"People are looking for something, something real, to fill that big soul gap."

Brehony uses real-life examples of midlife transitions, most culled from her psychotherapy practice at the Counseling Center in Roanoke from 1982 to 1988 and, more recently, in Virginia

Beach. (Names and identifying details have been changed to preserve anonymity).

■ Ask yourself two questions: "What did I most love to do when I was about 10 years old?" and "What would I do with my time if I won the lottery and was financially set for the rest of my life?" The answers provide great insight into what the soul craves, Brehony believes.

She suggests exploring some of the approaches that helped her, such as:

■ Dreams, "which are not random, they're there for a reason," Jung said dreams are like X-rays of the psyche, and Brehony suggests recording them and reflecting on them.

■ Find out what adds the most to your life, and what doesn't, and act accordingly. Boomers besieged with anxiety and depression are paying "for not living out our destinies; for being who society expects us to be. We pay for living a provisional life, devoid of passion, just getting by."

Living authentically may mean having fewer friendships than you used to, but having richer exchanges with the friends you do connect with. "I used to be a lot more extroverted than I am now," Brehony says. "I'm still an extrovert, but it's more focused.

"I say 'no' more than I used to, but I say 'yes' more often to things I wouldn't have before."

■ Practice some form of meditation, prayer, quiet time, reflection

or introspection every day.

Brehony's own dream had always been to try creative nonfiction. But she was scared to venture beyond the academic articles she had previously published. "For the same reason a lot of people put off their own creative destinies," she says. "Fear."

Quoting an Eastern mystic, she says: "The winds of grace are always blowing, but first we have to open the sail."

In other words, be awake to the possibilities around you.

People experiencing loss or a parent or a job or divorce find themselves hardest hit by midlife — "if you've only defined yourself by that particular role."

Coping with her own midlife crisis made her a stronger and more creative person, "but only after a lot of pain, reading and meditating," she says.

"It's a scary road, but all good myths take place in that dark spot. The people who go through life seemingly easily — without ever questioning their values and relationships — those are the people who come [through midlife] the worst. They're not awake."

Brehony's favorite metaphor for midlife is that of being on a boat: Each of us is driven by winds and tides we have no control over. But it doesn't mean we should lay in the bottom of the boat and eat bonbons.

"You can learn about your boat. You can pack for the trip, figure out how to use the winds and tides to go in the direction you're naturally supposed to go."

For Brehony, charting her own course means dividing time between her writing and her private practice in Virginia Beach. Her

next book is about ordinary people who do extraordinary things and, in the process, strengthen their communities.

Public service is also explored in "Awakening at Midlife" as a tool for bridging the midlife passage. "The best way to feel better about yourself is to do something for somebody else." Brehony says. "There is no end to the ways we can serve."

Judging by the response to the book — the first printing run is nearly sold out — boomers are finding companionship on her pages. At a recent book signing in Virginia Beach, a woman handed her a note detailing her pending divorce and wrote: "I know that God sent you to help me."

Another reader, a man, said to her: "You described my life perfectly. Have you been following me around for the last four years?"

The Roanoke Times, November 15, 1999, *continued*

The Roanoke Times, March 21, 1997